A REAL
Human Life

The Life of Jesus Christ IN You

MICHAEL J. WOLFE

WESTBOW
PRESS®
A DIVISION OF THOMAS NELSON
& ZONDERVAN

This book is a work of non-fiction. Unless otherwise noted, the author and the publisher make no explicit guarantees as to the accuracy of the information contained in this book and in some cases, names of people and places have been altered to protect their privacy.

WestBow Press books may be ordered through booksellers or by contacting:

WestBow Press
A Division of Thomas Nelson & Zondervan
1663 Liberty Drive
Bloomington, IN 47403
www.westbowpress.com
1 (866) 928-1240

Because of the dynamic nature of the Internet, any web addresses or links contained in this book may have changed since publication and may no longer be valid. The views expressed in this work are solely those of the author and do not necessarily reflect the views of the publisher, and the publisher hereby disclaims any responsibility for them.

ISBN: 978-1-9736-4468-2 (sc)
ISBN: 978-1-9736-4467-5 (hc)
ISBN: 978-1-9736-4469-9 (e)

Library of Congress Control Number: 2018913345

Print information available on the last page.

WestBow Press rev. date: 11/13/2018

Pastors, leaders, teachers, and regular believers have this to say about *A REAL Human Life:*

The book God gave Mike to write is so practical. The section on the sin nature is probably the most important piece of the book. It really helps explain the struggle with why we still sin. Mike put into words what I have never heard articulated, but it makes perfect sense. Logical!

Linda Sarver, retired educator
Milken National Educator 2003
Contributor to teacher's edition of *America,*
the Last Best Hope by Bill Bennett

Michael Wolfe is a man who writes with passion, like a man that has struck gold and wants to share his discovery to enrich others. These are truths that revolutionize our lives and turn our Christian living from mundane to an exciting adventure. He has discovered the truth that transforms – Christ IN you.

I think this book should be read by all who want to discover "the greatest life on the planet" and the potential of being enriched with every single blessing that God wants us to enjoy in our lives (Ephesians 1:3). If you are struggling to live the Christian life and long to discover the secret of the victorious life, this is the book you need to read.

Graham Stamford
Bible Teacher and Evangelist
Field Representative of Torchbearers
Founder of SportsReach

In a culture full of fake news, doctored photos and pseudo-science, Mike Wolfe has written something real. A Real Human Life gives real insight from a real person into the real way that Jesus can live in the hearts of His followers. With the care of a loving father and the wisdom of a seasoned pastor, Mike gives practical wisdom that serves as a biblical fact check for any Christian who wants to be real with Jesus and with others. If you're looking for a break from the fake, get into this book, and get back to the reality you were created to live.

Gregg Madsen
Pastor of Steadfast Gretna
Gretna, Nebraska

The truth of this book, so well defined and applied here, "is the plan and purpose of God for every person who believes." Are you struggling? Failing? Guilt-ridden? Defeated with shame or blame? On-again-off-again in your Christian life? Have you been working hard to reproduce the life of Jesus, as the Bible describes it? And, are you asking, "Why doesn't it work for me?" Then this book was written specifically for you. I pray that you will find it as helpful and motivating as I did.

R. Michael Huber, D. Min.
Founding consultant, Three Cords Coaching & Consulting
Retired President, Berean Fellowship of Churches

Contents

The artwork on the cover and the opening page of each chapter of *A REAL Human Life* is by the author's son, Brian Wolfe. The drawing was originally black and white in ink (Brian's usual medium). WestBow Press illustrators colorized the black and white drawing, with Brian's permission, and the resulting artwork was clearly the right choice for the book.

The drawing is inspired by Ezekiel 36:26

> And I will give you a new heart, a new spirit I will put within you. And I will remove the heart of stone from your flesh and give you a heart of flesh.

Brian has captured many features of that passage as it relates to the subject of this book. Christ *in* a human being is the key to this restored heart. The fire is a picture of the life of Jesus Christ igniting in what was formerly hard and dead. The explosion itself is a reminder that when the God of the Universe moves into a human life, dramatic change results.

Brian is on Instagram (brianthewolfe), where he regularly posts his drawings. He has also been a featured artist on blackworknow on Instagram.

The back cover photo of Michael Wolfe was provided by Andi Wagoner of Andi Wagoner Photography in Plattsmouth, Nebraska (Andi Wagoner Photography, LLC on Facebook).

Introduction

I started writing this book (actually putting it in Word files) on a sabbatical our church family – Plattsmouth Bible Church – sent Connie and me on in the summer of 2018. The overseers and church family, and others, graciously and generously gave us 3 months off after thirty plus years serving in ministry – a month for every 10 years. We traveled a lot – saw Crater Lake National Park and other Oregon-/northern California-related sites, spent a week in Oxford, UK seeing Stonehenge and Bath and other ancient sites, attended a Sunday church gathering in a church building where people have been meeting for nearly 1000 years, a ten-day tour of Israel which ignited great passion in both of us, seeing and experiencing the places Jesus and the apostles lived and wrote about, then back to England to visit Capernwray Hall, headquarters of a ministry started by a man who was/is a hero of the faith to me – Major W. Ian Thomas (more later on him), and then back to the United States for some other travel, family time, and work on our house. We are grateful to Plattsmouth Bible Church and all who helped us take this time for rest and renewal and reignition.

When we were in Oxford and on our way to Stonehenge and Bath, a person in our group – Tiffany from Australia – asked me what my book was about. It struck me, as I formulated an answer, that it would be a good thing to boil the point of this book down to some kind of statement. Connie helped me explain to Tiffany what it is about. I'm not sure where Tiffany stood with Jesus, but I'm pretty sure the topic was way outside her experience in life. So, not only is a brief explanation of the subject needed, but also needed within that explanation is some kind of "hook" to help believers and non-believers alike see and hear what they might receive from reading this book.

Here is that explanation: This book, *A REAL Human Life,* is meant to show human beings the kind of life *God* has always desired human beings to live.

In 2009, I preached a series on the Gospel of Luke at Plattsmouth Bible Church. I entitled that series "A REAL Human Life." I considered sifting through the notes and messages from that series to be the basis for this book. But as I started doing that, it began to sound like a commentary on the Gospel of Luke. There's nothing wrong with commentaries, I use them all the time. But I don't *read* them. They are for reference, not reading (unless you're kind of weird). The Gospel of Luke really demonstrates the human life of the Lord Jesus – as do the other Gospel accounts, but I did not want to write a commentary.

To help show how God desires human life to be lived by each human and *all* humans, the focus needed to be broader than the Gospel of Luke. So, here it is.

WHERE IT ALL STARTED

I was saved in 1976. God worked through some faithful believers in my hometown of Atlantic, Iowa, through a ministry called The Salt Cellar. This Christian coffee house (although I never once remember coffee being served), was opened as a way for youth to come to know Jesus Christ and begin growing in their faith. That was the impact of The Salt Cellar for me. I came to know Jesus Christ as Savior, and I began growing in my knowledge of Him, which is an *extremely* important part of life as a follower of Jesus. A number of the people listed in the Appreciation section were people who taught and led and helped me grow as God worked through them.

After graduating from high school in 1979, I went to what was then Grace College of the Bible in Omaha, Nebraska. My growth as a follower of Jesus continued because of my experience at Grace, but also – and this might be merely because I was eighteen to twenty-two years old – I developed what I now call "Bible College student syndrome." With the extremely limited knowledge I had about life and God's Word, the Bible, I treated what I had learned and was learning more as a weapon than a wound-healing treatment. I suffered from that syndrome for a number of years.

But God patiently and graciously introduced me to brothers in Christ whom He used for years to help me grow deeper in my faith and eventually away from the Bible college student syndrome problems from which I suffered. Some of these men were personal friends at Grace and later at Pleasantview Berean Church in Bellevue, Nebraska. Some of them were my teachers. A couple of them were "famous" people – one I met later and one, not.

In around 1981, I was introduced to the one I met later. Grace had a yearly Bible conference, and that year, one of the speakers was Major W. Ian Thomas. Major Thomas was an elderly British man with an interesting story, but mostly, a revolutionary, to my understanding, view of the "Christian" life. Also, during that week-long conference, I developed an affinity for listening to people with British accents.

So, here I was, a believer for five years, in my second or third year of Bible college, and I heard Major Thomas explain the Christian life as I had never heard it before. His messages have changed the course of my life ever since. I'll get to what he shared soon.

Later, as a youth pastor and minister of music at Pleasantview Berean Church, we invited Major Thomas to come speak for a Bible conference with our church family, likely around 1990. Unbelievably, to me, he came and shared the same message he had shared at Grace years before – the "Christian" life is Christ IN you. The Lord Jesus calls us to *that* life. The Lord Jesus demonstrated that life by His own earthly, human life. And, best of all, if the Lord Jesus lives His life in you, you don't have to *try* to live His life – He lives it.

And that last statement started me on a journey that continues to this day with the writing of this book. On the following pages, together, we will go through the Word of God, looking at what Jesus and the apostles say, asking questions, and seeking to apply their words to our own lives as literally as we can. By the way, I am an evangelical follower of Jesus, and, as such, I seek to read, study, interpret, and apply the Bible literally, grammatically, contextually, and historically. And something else to keep in mind throughout the book, I use the term "mankind" when referring to our entire race. I use "man" when referring to an individual male person.

Another person whom God used to cement these thoughts is a man I have never met. I have only read two books he wrote. David Needham wrote one book entitled *Birthright: Christian, Do You Know Who You Are?* Around the same time Major Thomas spoke at Grace, a group of us Bible college students and others read and studied *Birthright* together. The truths Needham shared in that book were on the same wavelength as Major Thomas. I hope the way I share the truth of Christ *in* you makes the reality of Christ in you accessible in a different way than Needham or Major Thomas. You should read *Birthright*. And *The Saving Life of Christ* by Major Thomas. And *Classic Christianity* by Bob George. *And* the excellent devotional Major Thomas wrote before he died – *The Indwelling Life of Christ.*

So, we will investigate and consider the idea that anything and everything Jesus Christ did on earth, He did as a human being, not as God. Uh oh! RED FLAG! Let me put your mind at ease. Jesus Christ certainly *is* God and was God in the flesh when He was on earth. We will address that issue as the book unfolds. But He lived as a human being and now He calls us human beings to live the *same* kind of life He lived: A REAL human life. He not only calls us to live that way, He makes it possible in the only way it *could* happen – HE lives the life.

I hope you don't merely enjoy reading *A REAL Human Life*, but that God uses this book to move you from *trying* to live the "Christian" life to what the Lord, through Major Thomas and David Needham and others, opened my eyes in 1981 – Jesus Christ living His life in you right now today – and everything that means for us. *We* can be REAL human beings, too.

CHAPTER 1
The Basis

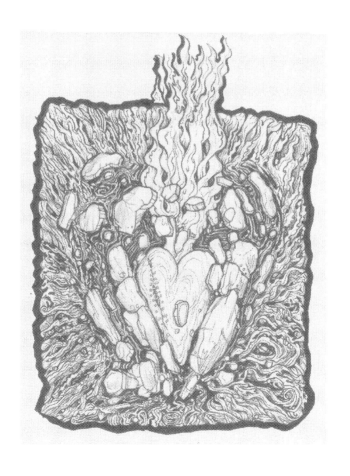

We need a definition for the word *real*. I am using the word to mean life as God intended life to be lived, actual, and as designed. It is real human life as God intended and designed life to be lived. God alone, the Creator of human life, has the right to define *real* human life.

Real also has antonyms. One opposite that helps me define *real* is *imitation*. An imitation life is not a life as God intended life to be lived. Imitation life is not actual life from God's perspective. Imitation life is not life as God designed it. Life without God's design is imitation and not real.

Both the Lord Jesus and the apostles say some very unusual things about real life, things that if true (and they *are* true), should cause us to stop and pay attention to what we think about these statements.

Jesus

> Truly, truly, I say to you, the Son can do nothing of His own accord, but only what He sees the Father doing. For whatever the Father does, the Son does likewise. (John 5:19)

> When you have lifted up the Son of Man, then you will know that I am He, and that I do nothing on My own authority, but speak just as the Father taught Me. And He who sent Me is with Me. He has not left Me alone, for I always do the things that are pleasing to Him. (John 8:28,29)

Even the fact that Jesus refers to Himself most often as "Son of Man" and not "Son of God" is significant to our discussion and consideration.

Jesus—the Way, the *Truth*, and the Life (John 14:6)—says that He can do *nothing* of His own accord. He can do *nothing* on His own authority, speaking *only* what the Father taught Him. Was He exaggerating? He can do nothing? How could someone who is God be unable to do anything on His own authority or of His own accord? That doesn't sound very *Godlike*, or *godly*, or *godish*. God is omnipotent, omnipresent, and omniscient. What could have happened in the Son of God to change those character qualities?

The Apostles

Really, nothing did change *in* Him. As God the Son, He was always who He had always been. But something the apostle Paul says in Philippians gives us some insight.

> Have this mind among yourselves, which is yours in Christ Jesus, who, though He was in the form of God, did not count equality with God a thing to be grasped, but emptied Himself, by taking the form of a servant, being born in the likeness of men. (Philippians 2:5–7)

Hebrews weighs in on this, too.

> Since therefore the children share in flesh and blood, He Himself likewise partook of the same things, that through death He might destroy the one who has the power of death, that is, the devil, and deliver all those who through fear of death were subject to lifelong slavery. For surely it is not angels that He helps, but He helps the offspring of Abraham. Therefore, He had to be made like His brothers in every respect, so that He might become a merciful and faithful High Priest in the

> service of God, to make propitiation for the sins of
> the people. For because He Himself has suffered
> when tempted, He is able to help those who are
> being tempted. (Hebrews 2:14–18)

What changed in the Lord Jesus was not who He was—God—
but *what* He was. He came to earth not as God but as *MAN*.
He emptied Himself—laid aside His God abilities—during His
time on earth in order to live a human life. He became the "Son
of Man." This is extremely significant! He came to earth for a
number of reasons, including the following, although the list is
not complete:

- to reveal the truth
- to live a *real* human life the way God always intended
  human life to be lived
- to die as the only effective, satisfactory sacrifice for
  mankind's sin
- to rise from the dead in order to open the way for mankind
  to experience *His* kind of life

And He did all of these things not as God but as *man*. God has
made it clear from the beginning (after sin came into mankind's
existence) what God's expectations and desires are. That's
the Law of Moses. Even if we take only the Big 10—the Ten
Commandments—they were never meant to be a way of salvation.
In fact, Romans 3:19–20 tells us clearly what the Law's purpose
was and is.

> Now we know that whatever the law says, it
> speaks to those who are under the law, so that
> every mouth may be stopped, and the whole world
> may be held accountable to God. For by the works
> of the Law *no human being will be justified in*

*His sight, since through the Law comes knowledge
of sin."*

The Law's purpose was never to justify—to save—anyone. Never.
The Law's purpose was to show us that we are sinners and in need
of a Savior. And it does its job really well.

Salvation and Justification in Christ

As we go forward, let's define some other terms.

Salvation: Evangelical believers (and most people) generally use
this term to define what happens when a person is rescued from
separation from God and being sent to hell, but then is restored to
fellowship and a relationship with God and an eternal destination
in heaven. Sounds good, doesn't it? It *is* good. But truthfully, I
think what was just described is more *justification.*

Look at *Romans 10:9,10.*

> If you confess with your mouth Jesus is Lord and
> believe in your heart that God raised Him from
> the dead, you will be saved. For with the heart one
> *believes and is justified,* and with the mouth one
> *confesses and is saved.*

Note that the actual word *salvation* is not even used there. *Saved*
could be an explanation of the whole process. Belief in the
resurrection of Jesus is tied directly to justification. Salvation is
tied to confession of Jesus as Lord when a person *is* justified.

So, to be saved, one must be justified by belief in the risen Jesus
and confess Jesus as Lord. I think this is tied tremendously to the
repeated words of John the Baptist, Jesus, and the apostles: "repent

and believe." In order for true belief to happen, the first step is to repent—to respond in obedience to the Spirit of God's work of conviction of sin and turn away from sin, self, and Satan. And nearly simultaneously, *confess* that Jesus is Master of one's life. Repentance and confession of Jesus as Lord are not some extra steps in the process of becoming a follower of Jesus. They are the first obedient actions of belief. "I turn away from myself (repent) and I submit to Jesus as Master." Then comes following Him and believing Him in every subsequent situation *to be* Master.

In order for the Lord Jesus to bring salvation—justification—to mankind, He had to live the kind of life that He lived—without sin and never breaking the Law. And He *did.* In fact, there are lots of words we could use to describe the life of the Lord Jesus, such as *model, substitute, example,* and *pattern.* I prefer the term *example.* His life as a human being is an example for the rest of us human beings regarding what human life was meant to be. If we need to know what a human life looks like—if we need an example—look at Him. And the basis of this book is that Jesus Christ was the only *real* human being ever. His example has tremendous application to our lives. Please keep reading!

But His example was not how justification and salvation came to us. Justification came to humanity by the substitutionary death of this Man Jesus—a real human being—who did life exactly how God intended and then stepped willingly into that death, and was then raised from the dead. And that resurrection—the risen life of Jesus—is also directly connected with salvation.

Look at *Romans 5:6–11* (Read this aloud, if you can, and emphasize the bold words.):

> For while we were still weak, at the right time
> Christ died for the ungodly [that's us]. For one

will scarcely die for a righteous person—though perhaps for a good person one would dare even to die—but **God** shows His love for **us** in that **while we were still sinners,** Christ died for **us.** Since, therefore, we have now been **justified** by His blood, much more shall we be **saved** by Him from the wrath of God. For if, while we were **enemies,** we were **reconciled** to God **by the death of His Son,** much more, now that we **are** reconciled, shall we be **saved by His life.** More than *that,* we also rejoice in God through our Lord Jesus Christ, through whom we have now **received** reconciliation.

Our lives are saved through *His* life—His *resurrected* life—once we have been justified through His *death.* His death, when we confess He *is* our Master and repent of our own efforts to save ourselves, justifies us. His *life* saves us. *His* life *saves us.*

What kind of situation could lead to a person needing to be physically saved? Maybe a person is drowning or trapped in a burning house or a crushed car or attacked by a wild animal. If a person is saved in one of those circumstances, somehow he or she is rescued. And then what happens? The rescued person's life is *saved.* Danger is averted. But that's not all. The person's life is now back in play. Every moment after *that* moment is a moment that would not have happened if the person's life had not been *saved.*

The risen life of the Lord Jesus Christ is what saves our lives when we repent and believe. Every moment after *that* moment of rescue from sin and death is a moment that would not have happened in a relationship with God if our lives had not been *saved.* Being saved is, yes, going to heaven someday – and I am not downplaying that.

But being saved is more accurately having *this* life – day to day, right now – rescued by the God who made salvation happen.

Look at *Romans 8:10,11* (again, read the bold words with emphasis):

> But if Christ is **in** you, although the body is **dead because of sin**, the Spirit is **life because of righteousness**. If the Spirit of Him who raised Jesus from the dead dwells **in** you, He who raised Christ Jesus from the dead will **also** give **life** to your mortal bodies through His Spirit who **dwells in you**.

The body is dead. Earlier in Romans 7, Paul had made it clear that the mortal body, the flesh of mankind, is open to sin and is the doorway for sin *into* the believer. And it is frustrating and maddening. But these dead bodies – "bod[ies] of death" (Romans 7:24) – are made *alive* through the indwelling Spirit of God in those who repent and believe in Jesus Christ (Romans 8:11). The resurrected life of Jesus lived by the indwelling Spirit of God *in* believers raises their mortal bodies from the dead. Our lives are saved right now by His life.

On this basis, we will continue to look at *real* human life the way God intends it for humanity – *for us* – for you and me!

CHAPTER 2
Christ In You

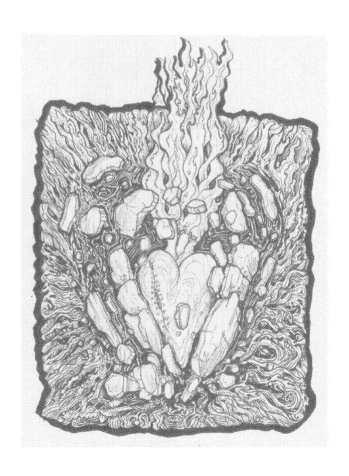

The words "Christ in you" have likely been both encouraging and frustrating to followers of Jesus over the years. I don't think too many would argue that God says our Christian lives are characterized, or should be, by Christ *in* us. But the fact that we rarely experience Him in our lives is discouraging and disappointing, maybe even depressing. We can see, and we know, that's what God is thinking, what God wants, and what God claims is possible, but we often ask, "Why do I not see it?"

The Gospel

Consider *Romans 1:16,17.*

> I am not ashamed of the gospel, for it is the power of God for salvation to everyone who believes, to the Jew first and also to the Greek. For in it the righteousness of God is revealed from faith to faith, as it is written, "The righteous shall live by faith."

The focus of the book of Romans is the impact of the gospel on the lives of people who believe the gospel. And note the two aspects of the gospel's work, salvation and righteousness. The gospel is *God's* power for salvation. Refer back to Chapter 2 regarding what salvation is. The gospel is *God's* power – not *our* power, not our brilliance, not our methods or devices. If a person hears the gospel and believes, it is the work of God alone. And when that rescue of a lost person happens, those of us who watch and share that time with the newly-saved person can rejoice even more because we have actually seen the power of God at work. God Himself in action doing what only He can do. Amazing!

Also, in the gospel, the righteousness of God is revealed. Through the gospel, salvation comes through the power of God and God's righteousness is revealed *in* people who believe the gospel. Not man's righteousness – *God's*. I find it extremely interesting that Christians put so much emphasis on getting saved (escaping sin and hell) and miss the resulting impact of that deliverance – God's righteousness in life. Even the book of Romans itself makes this clear. The words "salvation" and "saved" are mentioned thirteen times in Romans. The word "righteousness" is mentioned thirty-nine times. Three times more mention of righteousness than salvation. When a person comes to faith in Jesus Christ and goes from being lost to being found, from being dead to being alive, the next gospel work that should be visible is God's righteousness starting to show through that person's life. This might be where we start to get frustrated. We *don't* see it. God says this should be the result of the gospel, but most of the time, we see exactly what we always saw in our lives before the gospel came in. Is God lying? Am I not trying hard enough? What am I doing wrong that keeps me from seeing God's righteousness?

Those are important questions. Can you, can I, live anyone else's life? Can I live your life? Could I live some famous person's life (see Chapter 7 about Mike and Mike)? Can I live the life of Jesus Christ? No. Can I produce the righteousness of God? No. What *can* I do? First, that's not a good question. We all know that "all our righteousness is as filthy rags" (Isaiah 64:6). "All have sinned and fall short of the glory of God" (Romans 3:23). "There is none righteous, not even one" (Romans 3:10). How can God expect us – you and me – to produce His righteousness, knowing what He knows about us?

Good News!

Here's good news! *He does not expect us to produce His righteousness.* Well, isn't that what Romans 1:17 says we are supposed to see in our lives? Romans 1:17 does *not* say, "Produce righteousness in your life because you are a believer." It says that the work of the gospel in believers is *God's* righteousness. And only God Himself can produce His righteousness. "What *can* I do?" is not a good question because there is nothing we can do to produce God's righteousness.

A better question is, "What can *Christ* do?" None of our works of righteousness bring about the results God is looking for (see Titus 3:5). Only God produces those results. And He has worked through the gospel to bring salvation to us who believe – rescue from sin and the flesh and the devil – which puts us in the place where *He* can produce His righteousness. It is not what you or I *do*, it is who you and I *are* and whom you and I *know*. It is all Jesus Christ.

Ephesians speaks directly to who we now are in Christ and how He has put us in a place where He is free to be Himself with no restrictions. From now on, continue to read words in bold with emphasis.

> Blessed be the God and Father of our Lord Jesus Christ, who has blessed us **in Christ** with **every** spiritual blessing in the heavenly places, even as He chose us **in Him** before the foundation of the world, that we should **be holy and blameless** before Him. **In love, He** predestined us for **adoption to Himself as sons through Jesus Christ**, according to the purpose of **His** will. (Ephesians 1:3-5)

Let's stop there and consider what God just told us. God has blessed us who believe with *every* spiritual blessing in the heavenly places. Name a spiritual blessing that God has not blessed us with. You can't do it – He has blessed us with *every* blessing through Jesus Christ. God is holding nothing back from us. And He chose us in Christ before the world was even formed for a reason: So that *we* should be holy and blameless before Him. Not merely before Him when we get to heaven someday, but holy and blameless right now in this life.

"Well, what about 'the heavenly places' part? Isn't this talking only about when we get to heaven someday?" Probably, but I don't think it waits until then, looking at the broader context of Scripture. Mankind was created in God's image and likeness, male and female, for what reason? To look like Him only in heaven *someday*? NO! – to look like Him *every* day of our existence. Mankind bears the image of God to demonstrate who God is. And now, through the life, death, and resurrection of Jesus Christ, and the subsequent indwelling of the Spirit of God *in* believers, we are once again those through whom God can show Himself.

He chose us to be holy and blameless, and in love, He adopted us as sons – children. When an adoption takes place, the resulting legal arrangement is that the adopted child is in that family, taking the family name, enveloped in the love and activity of the family. Human adoption fails from time to time. But God, the perfect Father (Father as father is meant to be) looks at His adopted children and each individual child and declares that child's family name is now His name – "I AM." This is not to say we become gods. There is only one God. But, if God had a last name, and you and I have been adopted into His family as His children, His name is *our* name. And who He *is* is whom He desires us to show.

Eyes Wide Open

God came into this relationship with His eyes wide open. He knows our struggle with the flesh in this life on earth (and we will spend more time soon looking at dealing with the flesh). He has made it entirely possible, though, for you and me to experience the same life Jesus experienced *because* Jesus Christ lives *in* us through the indwelling Spirit. Jesus lived human life as the Father lived by the Father living in Him (see John 17:21). Jesus prayed in John 17 that *we* would live in Him in the same way He lived in the Father, Him living His life *in* us showing Himself *through* us. It is Christ IN you (Colossians 1:27). I live, but not me, it is CHRIST who lives IN me – by faith in Him (Galatians 2:20).

We are new creations in Christ Jesus, now able to be filled with Christ Jesus Himself. Like jars of clay, we are now useful to the Potter who made us. A believer in Jesus Christ is no longer what he or she was but is what and *whom* God makes him or her. As Ephesians 1 continues, focus on these spiritual blessings God has blessed us with, to the praise of His glory.

> In Him we have **redemption** through **His** blood, the **forgiveness of our trespasses**, according to the riches of **His** grace, which **He** lavished upon us, in all wisdom and insight **making known** to us the mystery of **His will**, according to **His** purpose which **He** set forth **in Christ** as a plan for the fullness of time, to unite all things **in Him**, things in heaven and things on earth. **In Him** we have obtained **an inheritance**, having been **predestined** according to the purpose **of Him** who works all things according to the counsel of **His will**, so that we who were the first to hope in Christ might be to the praise of **His glory**. **In Him** you also, when you heard the word of truth, the gospel of your salvation, and believed in **Him**, were **sealed with the promised Holy Spirit**, who is the **guarantee** of our inheritance until we acquire possession of it, to the praise of **His glory**. (Ephesians 1:7-14)

WOW! *In* Christ, we have redemption, we have forgiveness, we know God's will, we have an inheritance (Romans 8:17 says that we are fellow heirs with Christ), we have been predestined to be to the praise of His glory, we were sealed with the Spirit as a guarantee *of* that inheritance. All of these spiritual blessings come to us *in Christ* because of who we now are by God's power.

There's more!

> For this reason, because I have heard of your faith in the Lord Jesus and your love toward all the saints, I do not cease to give thanks for you, remembering you in my prayers, that the God of our Lord Jesus Christ, the Father of glory, may give you the Spirit of wisdom and of revelation in the **knowledge of Him**, having the eyes of your hearts enlightened, that you may **know** what is **the hope to which He has called you**, what are **the riches of His glorious inheritance in the saints**, and **what is the immeasurable greatness of His power toward us who believe**, according to the working of **His** great might that **He** worked **in Christ** when **He raised Him from the dead** and **seated Him at His right hand** in the heavenly places, far above all rule and authority and power and dominion, and above every name that is named, not only in this age but also in the one to come. And He put all things under His feet and **gave Him as head over all things to the church**, which **is His body**, the **fullness of Him** who fills all in all. (Ephesians 1:15-23)

Paul prays that his readers (and I pray that mine) may be given the Spirit of wisdom and revelation in the knowledge of Christ.

Knowing Christ is eternal life (John 17:3). And in knowing Him, we know the hope to which He has called us (restoration to Him and His righteousness seen in us). In knowing Him, we know the riches of *His* glorious inheritance –Christ's inheritance, which, as we mentioned referring to Romans 8:17, is *our* inheritance. This is what Paul means when he writes, "…in the saints." When Jesus Christ lives His life in us through the indwelling Spirit, we can expect His inheritance to be ours by His power working in us. What is His is ours. Amazing! And then, in knowing Christ, we know the immeasurable greatness of His power toward us who believe. And Paul goes on to explain that a little further. It is *His* power, *His* work, *in* Christ, the same power that raised Christ Jesus from the dead and seated Him at God's own right hand.

Did you catch that one? God desires to use the same power *in you* through Christ that He used to *raise* Christ Jesus from the dead. That sounds *nothing* like going through life defeated and discouraged because we can't figure out how to produce God's righteousness in ourselves. That sounds *nothing* like a group of Christians gathering on Sunday morning and singing without excitement, sitting passively in a pew or on a chair with nothing to celebrate. If God puts the same dynamite power (the Greek word is "*dunamis*") into our daily lives that He used to raise Jesus Christ from the dead, I would expect that we would stand out in our communities and our culture like sore thumbs. And then we could share with them, "It's not me! It's *Jesus*! I cannot do anything. This is the power of *God* working through His Spirit, living the risen life of Jesus Christ in me. Do you want that for yourself!?"

Imagine Tha …

I almost wrote, "Imagine that!" But we don't have to imagine that kind of life – we see it in real people in the Scripture in addition to Jesus: Peter, Paul, John, Barnabas, Philip, Silas, Titus, Timothy, and on and on. You might say, "Yeah, Mike, but those are *Bible people*." Do you realize the misinformation that would cause you or anyone to say that? People are people and it doesn't matter if a person got his or her name in the Bible. All human beings struggle and fail and sometimes seem to get it right. But the people who trust Jesus and do what He says, *do* stand out because God is seen through them. I certainly believe that the Bible is complete with the 66 books included in it. But I also have realized that the book of Acts – the acts of the Spirit in the lives of people who trust Jesus – is still being written every day of the week. *We can experience Christ in us just like Bible people did.* We have the same Spirit of God living the same life of Jesus Christ who lives the same life of the Father that He has *always* lived. No difference. History is full of people whose names are *not* in the Bible who showed Christ in them - Martin Luther, Dietrich Bonhoeffer, Corrie Ten Boom, Ian Thomas, Stuart Briscoe, J. Vernon McGee, Charles Stanley, Francis Chan, David Platt, and on and on.

When Christ is in you or me or anyone, His life is what comes out. *His* life, not our lives trying to look like His life. We cannot live any other person's life, especially Jesus Christ's. *He* has to live it. We'll talk later about getting out of His way. But first, in the next chapter, I want to make something crystal clear about who *gets* to live His life. It's not everybody – although it *could* be.

CHAPTER 3
How Does Christ Get IN You?

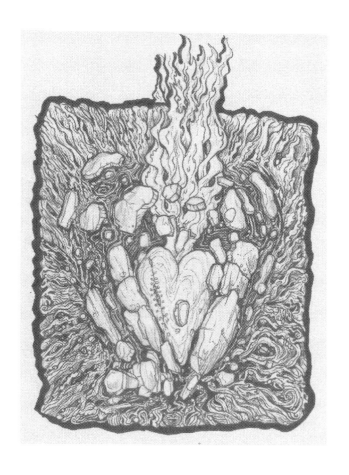

The placement of this chapter was a big question. One thing that scares me, as a person who has been called by God to speak and proclaim God's Word in public, is the possibility of getting something wrong. James 3 tells us that teachers will be "judged with greater strictness." Whatever that means, it certainly motivates me to teach the principles and words of God as accurately as I can. Thankfully for all of us who believe in Jesus Christ, we have the indwelling Spirit of God who knows and teaches us God's Word. But there are false teachers out there. And sometimes false thinking in our own minds. Either of those could cause us to get off-base. O Lord! Please protect me and my readers from that!

For Whom is This Book Written?

The reason I bring all that up is that we have been laying out the Scriptural concept of Christ living His life in you. Anyone could pick up this book or download it and assume that it was automatically talking to and about him or her. I want to make it clear that this book is for people who not merely "believe in God" or have "found God," but for people who have put their trust in Jesus Christ alone for forgiveness of sin and restoration to life. This book is for people who actually and fully believe in Jesus Christ and *follow* Him – trust Him and obey Him.

Should this chapter have come earlier, maybe as the introduction? If it had been in the introduction, lots of people would skip it. *Don't skip this!* And, by the way, if you skipped the introduction, go back and read it. There's important stuff there!

I'm not trying to make anybody mad or discourage anyone – far from it! But don't assume that *you are* a believer in and a follower of Jesus. If the descriptions of who this book is written for do not really describe you, I want to share with you what it means to *be* a believer in and a follower of Jesus Christ. Even if you can pinpoint a date or experience when you did believe, please don't skip this chapter. Pretend that you have never heard it before and allow the Spirit of God to do His work. Especially if you are looking at your Christian life and not seeing the righteousness of God or the life of Jesus demonstrated through you. Francis Chan, in his book *Crazy Love*, asks us to consider – if you read the Bible for the first time, would you think current-day Christianity and the church look like what you saw as you read?

When I first started in ministry at Pleasantview Berean Church in Bellevue, Nebraska, I worked with a senior pastor named James Jost. James had an older brother named Gene. James and Gene became believers during the Jesus Movement of the late 1960s and early 1970s. James told the story of Gene, freshly saved and eager to grow in his faith, showing up at a Sunday morning church service – all the churchgoers prim and proper, and Gene with his hippie attire and youthful zeal – and in the middle of the church service stood up with his open Bible and asked, "When does *this stuff* start happening!?"

That story has stuck with me for many years – and has kind of spurred me on to experience the life of Jesus Christ in the way *Jesus* talks about. In order for anything of Jesus to happen in the life of a human being, there has to be real change *from* Jesus *in* that human being. The way that change happens is part of what the Bible refers to as the gospel.

There are many ways to express and share the gospel. The method shared here has been very meaningful to me because it includes what Romans 1:16,17 lays out as the two dramatic issues affected by the gospel. "I am not ashamed of the gospel, for it is **God's power for salvation** to all who believe, to the Jew first and also to the Greek. For in it, **the righteousness of God is revealed** from faith to faith, just as it is written, 'The righteous will live by faith.'"

The two issues are salvation from sin and the righteousness of God. The gospel message works in both of those arenas. Many church people would say that the gospel is how to get saved – and I don't disagree with that. But the gospel is also how to *live* saved – the righteousness of God being shown and demonstrated in the lives of those who are saved. So, even before we get to my favorite gospel-sharing method, let me ask: Has the gospel in *you* been doing its work of bringing salvation from sin and demonstrating God's righteousness? Does *your* life look like Jesus? This chapter is for you.

The Three Circles

I'm going to share what was taught to me as "The 3 Circles." I am grateful to David Kaufmann of City Church Network in Nashville, Tennessee for sharing it with me.

We read in the Bible that God created mankind with specific things in mind. God's design was for mankind to live God's way – in a perfect relationship with God and a perfect relationship with others. Jesus later revealed clearly what that perfect relationship is – LOVE.

> You shall love the Lord your God with all your heart and with all your soul and with all your mind. This is the great and first commandment. And the second is like it: You shall love your neighbor as yourself. On these two commandments depend all the Law and the Prophets." (Matthew 22:37-40)

The Bible tells us much more about God's design and God's way. But mankind ruined God's design by a single act. Sin was introduced into mankind's existence when the first man, Adam, decided to go his *own* way instead of God's. Don't worry about whether it was Eve's fault or Adam's – they were both there and Adam did not say a word. It was primarily Adam's responsibility. Anyway, that's not the issue here. The issue is that sin separated mankind from God as mankind pursued our own way instead of God's. Separation from God was not God's original design. He desired to be with us. He *still* desires to be *with* us. But sin ruined that and now mankind is broken.

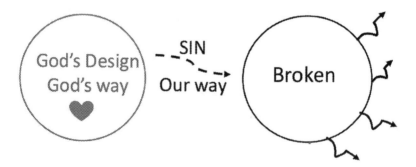

Mankind attempts to fix our brokenness by all kinds of activity. The wiggly arrows represent things like drugs, alcohol, money, sex and relationships, and even church activity and spiritual pursuits.

There are lots of problems with these attempts and you can see it in the diagram that none of those activities is going God's way. They are all going mankind's way – *away* from God. And the "wiggliness" of the arrows shows that at some point, like bungee cords, they will snap us back to the reality of brokenness. That reality is that broken cannot fix brokenness. But God knew all this when He made us. He was ready, willing, and able to deal with it.

The third circle shows the only effective action to rescue mankind from separation and brokenness. God Himself went into action to fix our sin problem and restore us to His design. God sent Jesus to earth as a human being to live the way God designed human beings to live. And Jesus did it (this is the down arrow on the left). Since Jesus lived God's way, according to God's design, He is the only one qualified to make the payment God requires for sin. We see a picture of that requirement in the Old Testament Law: a spotless sacrifice had to die. Jesus *was* that spotless sacrifice, having never sinned or disobeyed God. The cross in the middle represents His death, which can and does overrule sin in mankind. But His death was not the end of the story. The up arrow on the right represents the resurrection of Jesus Christ from the dead, the very thing that allows mankind's access back to the kind of life God designed for us. This circle represents the gospel.

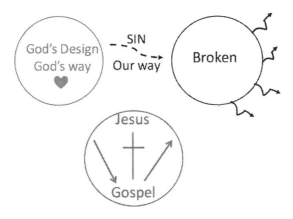

As you look at the circle of God's design and God's way on the left – love God and love others – and then the circle marked "broken" on the right, which circle describes you and what your life demonstrates? Don't give yourself more credit than you deserve. Warm feelings and desires are not the same thing as action and reality.

For some reading this, if you are honest, the broken circle is probably what you see coming out of your life. Going away from God, pursuing your own way and your own solutions, even if you want to be fixed.

What must happen to take advantage of the only solution provided to fix this brokenness? We must *turn* and go God's direction. The biblical word for turn is repent – stop going one direction and turn around to go the other direction. Stop going our own way, turn and go God's way. And in the diagram, there's another word with repent – BELIEVE. We turn from our way and go God's way by believing the gospel.

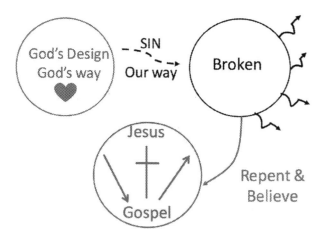

Because of the death of Jesus Christ and His resurrection from the dead, those who repent and believe God's solution to our separation and brokenness can now recover God's design and pursue life God's way.

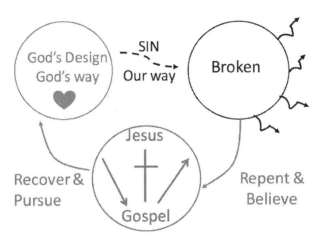

All of this was and is God's work – the gospel is *God's* power for salvation. There is nothing any person can do to fix our brokenness – only God can fix us through Jesus Christ.

So, what is your response to this explanation of sin and salvation? No one finds God – God finds people and rescues them (remember the shepherd who leaves 99 sheep to find one that is lost, Matthew 18:12-14). No one "asks Jesus into his or her heart." According to Ezekiel and Jeremiah, and Jesus, and Paul, *God* changes people's hearts from dead to alive. Yes, Revelation 3:20 – "Behold, I stand at the door and knock. If anyone hears My voice and opens the door, I will come in to him and eat with him and he with Me." But don't allow yourself to soften that passage – this is not a passive "coming into one's heart." This is Jesus coming into a person's life and being directly involved in every aspect of life from the inside out.

Are you truly a believer and a follower of Jesus? Does your life, and do your subsequent actions, show obedience to Him in all areas – your living situation, your sex life, your work life, your entertainment life – *all* areas? If your honest answer is "no," what's the solution? *Repent and believe!* No matter *what* you have said or thought about your spiritual life. Trust God and do what He says – that's equivalent to "repent and believe." By the way, that is what God has always desired from mankind – trust Me and do what I say. When a human being repents and believes, recovering and pursuing God's design for his or her life, the Spirit – God Himself – moves in to that life, living the life of Jesus Christ in the one who believes: God's work accomplished by God Himself.

Respond now. Tell God that you have been trying to fix your own sin problem. You now realize you cannot do it. Only *He* can do it – and He *has* done it through Jesus Christ. Intentionally turn away from your own efforts and believe in Jesus Christ and what He has done to rescue you through His life, death, and resurrection. Something not included on the 3 Circles diagram, but something that shows how the life of Jesus is lived in a human being, is that the Spirit of God comes in and lives the life of Jesus Christ in those who repent and believe. That's the crowning jewel of the gospel – we don't even have to *try* to live it. Only God can and only God does.

CHAPTER 4
You're Going to Want This Chapter To NEVER End!

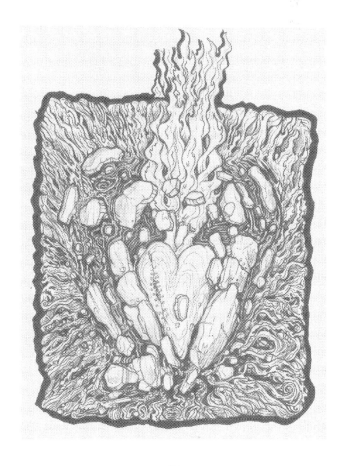

When I was a young believer, I bought a lot of books. Not because I read them. In fact, I have a hard time reading. But I bought them because I liked the look of books. I thought having books made me look smart. Abe Penner, my New Testament Survey teacher at Grace College of the Bible, had so many books in his office that they were piled on shelves, stacked on the floor, covering his desk – everywhere! He told us first-year Bible college students that people had asked him, "Have you *read* all those books?" And his answer was, "Some twice!"

There are lots of books about lots of topics, but I often have been drawn to books that dealt with difficult passages in Scripture. And some of those, I actually tried to read!

The Bible Says That!?

In this chapter and the next, I will take us through a number of Scripture passages that might be considered difficult. But as I view them from the perspective of Christ living His life in me/ in anyone, I find a lot of the difficulty fades away. I warn you, I come to these passages – and also, much of life – from the perspective that if a child can understand it, that might be the way it is supposed to be understood (based on the words of the Lord Jesus and having faith like children).

The passages in this chapter are focused on the little five-chapter book of 1 John. In 1 John, some difficult things are addressed that relate directly to the theme of Christ in you. Chuck Swindoll, introducing his study of 1 John on the radio in his later years, mentioned that he had never yet taught 1 John because of the great difficulty he saw in the book. I don't know for certain where Chuck Swindoll is with the concept of the indwelling life of Christ, but I find 1 John a huge encouragement *because* of those difficult passages. But don't misunderstand me! Chuck Swindoll has been teaching God's Word for many years, quite effectively – I am no Chuck Swindoll. This realization nearly put this book to a stop! But the Spirit of God has moved me to write, so I have written so that He can use what is in this book to help and encourage and revolutionize the lives of those He is preparing to read it, so that He can be seen in us.

> This is the message we have heard from Him and proclaim to you, that God is light, and **in Him** is no darkness at all. If we say we have fellowship with Him while we walk in darkness, we lie and do not practice the truth. But if we walk in the light, as He is in the light, we have fellowship with one another, and the blood of Jesus His Son cleanses us from all sin. If we say we have no sin, we deceive ourselves, and the truth is not in us. If we confess our sins, He is faithful and just to forgive us our sins and to cleanse us from all unrighteousness. If we say we have not sinned, we make Him a liar, and His word is not in us. (1 John 1:5-10)

Included in this passage are some big words like "all" and "lie" or "liar." Also included are sentences that bring out some things that exclude other things – if this, then that – if not this, then not that. We will take this passage apart and show the gigantic hope lying in it.

"God is light and in Him is no darkness at all." There is probably not a lot of disagreement about this truth. Not a lot until He follows it up with, "If we say we have fellowship with Him and walk in darkness, we lie and do not practice the truth." Light and darkness really have no fellowship together. Light overpowers darkness. I heard this illustration somewhere: When you open a closet door, why doesn't the darkness of the closet pour out into the lighted room? It doesn't – the light pours *into* the darkness. Light overpowers darkness. If we say we have fellowship with God the Light, yet live in *darkness*, we're lying – the truth cannot be in us. Darkness and light cannot co-exist.

"What about sunlight and shadow? Aren't those two co-existing?" Not at all. Shadow could not and would not exist without light. As Switchfoot so eloquently put in a song years ago, " …the shadow *proves* the sunshine." Shadow is not the absence of light. When the moon is in the earth's shadow, it can still be seen. God says in 1 John that He is Light and in Him there *is no darkness*. So, for us who believe to be *in Him*, we cannot walk in darkness. What does "walk" mean? It means to live, exist, operate, move forward. Darkness cannot describe the life of a true follower of Jesus because He is *light*. The Light of the World living in a human being produces what? Darkness? NO – that's CRAZY! He produces *light*!

Light and Darkness

Do you see light coming out of your life? "In Him was life and the life was the light of men. The light shines in darkness, and the darkness has not overcome it." (John 1:4,5) Do you see the life of the Light of the World demonstrated in your life? Stop trying to produce what only *He* can! Repent! Turn away from your own efforts. Submit and yield yourself to Him. Deny yourself, say no to those things that keep Him from being Him in you.

"But if we walk in the light, as He is in the light, we have fellowship with one another" (1 John 1:7). Is John telling us that if we *can* produce God's kind of light in ourselves like God does, then we can be in fellowship with God? That's ridiculous! Only God, who *is* Light, can produce light. If we walk in the light, as He is in the light, we are experiencing *Him in us*. He is showing Himself through our lives. His character of light is seen coming out of our lives by His power. And the blood of Jesus, God's Son, cleanses us from *all* sin. If it is *me* producing light and fellowship with God, then it also has to be something I did to bring about the cleansing from sin through the blood of Jesus. Once again, ridiculous!

In the same way the light produced in the life of a follower of Jesus is God Himself showing in that life, so, too, it is His work through the blood of Jesus Christ that cleanses us from all sin. *All* sin. All sin is cleansed by His blood, in those who believe in Jesus Christ for forgiveness of sin. Verse 8 addresses a person who hears that wonderful truth, but responds, "I'm no sinner! I don't sin! I have never sinned!" That person is deceived, and the truth is not in that person. That person is not yet saved.

But verses 9 and 10 keep clearing things up for us. "If we confess our sins," [if we agree with God that sin is nothing like Him, so it could not possibly be like us in whom He lives], "He is faithful and just to forgive us our sins and to cleanse us from all unrighteousness." When a person understands that we are freed from sin's power and from sin's consequences through Jesus Christ, and we agree with God about how awful sin is, we then understand deeply, fully, and clearly how faithful and just God has been to forgive us *and* to cleanse us. Before the work of Jesus on the cross and His blood shed for me and my sins, I completely deserved death, separation, brokenness, and everything that came with sin. But now, realizing who God is and what He has done, I can see His faithfulness and justice. I can see what tremendous immeasurable riches and blessings He has blessed me with in Christ Jesus.

"If *we* say we have not sinned, *we* make Him a liar," [something that is impossible – us making Him a liar] "and His Word is not in us." For a person to say he or she has not sinned is a lie and a demonstration that the Word of God has no home in the person who says it.

In the Same Way

The next difficult passage follows immediately after the previous one in 1 John.

> My little children, I am writing these things to you **so that you may not sin**. But if anyone does sin, we have an Advocate with the Father, Jesus Christ, the righteous. He is the propitiation for our sins, and not for ours only but also for the sins of the whole world. And by this we know that we have come to know Him, if we keep His commandments. Whoever says, 'I know Him,' but does not keep His commandments is a liar, and the truth is not in him, but whoever keeps His word, in Him truly the love of God is perfected. By this we may know that we are in Him: whoever says he abides in Him **ought to walk in the same way in which He walked**. (1 John 2:1-6)

The statement in 1 John 2:1 is like a stick of dynamite! John, under the inspiration of the Spirit of God – God Himself – tells us that he wrote this little five-chapter letter *so that we may not sin*! So God Himself through John is telling us that He had this written down so that we may not sin. Did He not *just* say that if anyone claims to be without sin, that person is a liar and the truth is not in him? What gives?

It is not specifically spelled out here, but, in context with the rest of Scripture, it is clear that the only way for human beings to live without sin is for Jesus Christ to live *His* sinless life in them. It could not and would not be their doing, it would be the life of Jesus Christ. He is the one to be congratulated. He is the one to be revered and extolled.

And notice something else – back in 1 John 1:5-10. "If we SAY …" "If we SAY …" "If we SAY …" *Saying* is not the thing to look at in a person. *Doing* is. And if a human being gets through one hour, one minute, one second without sinning, it is pretty clear that it would not be acceptable to start talking about it, saying, "I just lived one second without sinning!" Because no human being *can* live that way. Only Jesus can. And tooting one's own horn is pride, which is sin.

"I am writing these things so that you may not sin," is followed by a caveat. "But if anyone does sin, we have an Advocate with the Father, Jesus Christ, the righteous." John, just like Paul in Romans 7, is fully cognizant that human beings will sin, even when specifically devoting themselves as fully as possible to the Lord Jesus. But when we *do* sin, we have a great advantage. We have a defense attorney who argues our case from a unique perspective. He argues from the perspective that He Himself has paid the satisfactory payment for the crimes we committed. He knows our case from beginning to end, because He endured the depths of not just the sin we committed, but the wrath of God against that sin. He Himself endured the separation from God that we have to endure: "My God! My God! Why have You forsaken Me!" For the first time in His eternal existence, Jesus knew what it felt like and what it *was* like to be separated from God the Father (Mark 15:34). Yes, Jesus Christ the righteous one advocates for us who believe.

His death satisfied the debt God owed us for sin which is death. "The wages of sin is death" (Romans 6:23). That's "propitiation." And look what it says as verse 2 continues, "…not for our sins only," [those of us who believe in Jesus Christ], "but for the sins of the whole world." Does this mean that everyone gets a free pass? Everyone goes to heaven? No, not in the least. The rest of Scripture is still in effect including John 1:12, "To those who received Him He gave the right to become children of God, to those who believed in His name." Everyone's sins are dealt with and can be removed because of the death of Jesus Christ. But it still requires the response of belief and receiving the gift of justification through Jesus Christ. Obviously, not everyone will receive that gift. But it is totally available to every person. "God is not willing that *any* should perish, but that *all* should come to repentance." (2 Peter 3:9)

Verse 3 of chapter 2 in 1 John, " …by this we know that we have come to know Him, if we keep His commandments." And then, a few words later, in verse 5, " …but whoever keeps His commandments, in him truly the love of God is perfected." The point here is that there is evidence of the God of the universe moving in to the life of a human being: not only the light of God, not only the sinless life of Jesus being apparent, but obedience to the commands of God. If we keep His commandments, we can know that we *have* come to know Him.

Isn't that kind of a funny way to say that, "by this we *know* that we have come to know Him?" If I, a person who wants desperately to know Him and to experience Him in my lowly life, see that I am keeping His commandments, I can know that I know Him. We have already seen that the Law is in place to show us that we are sinners and not to bring us salvation. The Law shows us our need of the Savior. So when, by the power of the risen Jesus Christ, I see obedience to His commands in my life, I know that it is *Him* doing it. I have proven over and over in my life that I cannot do it, but He proved and continues to prove that He *can* and *does!*

On the other hand, John continues, whoever says, "I know Him" but does not keep His commandments is a liar – the truth is not in that person. Jesus is not *in* that person, because Jesus will keep His own commandments.

And then, back to verse 5, whoever keeps His word (same as "commandments"), in *that* person, God's love is perfected. God's love is completed or brought to fullness. It is so very clear that it cannot come from you or me or any human effort. In order for the love of God to be brought to full completion and perfection in a human being requires that God Himself is the one doing it. And then, verse 6 – here's another way to know we are in Him – if I say I abide in Him, my life ought to look exactly like His, because it is *His life* being lived. He lives His life in those who believe. He obeys His own commands in those who believe. He lives without sin in those who believe. He produces light in those who believe. All HIM.

The World and Its Things

Next difficult passage – *1 John 2:15-17*:

> Do not love the world or the things in the world. If anyone loves the world, the love of the Father is not in him. For all that is in the world – the desires of the flesh and the desires of the eyes and the pride of life – is not from the Father but is from the world. And the world is passing away along with its desires, but whoever does the will of God abides forever.

Clearly, followers of Jesus are here on earth to love lost people so this is not talking about rejecting the people around us who do not know, love, or follow Jesus. This is speaking of the world's *system*, the ways of the world, the things of the world. Do not love that. Do not place any hope or expectation in that. Do not live for that. If you or I or anyone loves something that is not God Himself, places hope or expectation in that thing, and lives for that thing, what is that person called? An idol worshiper, not a God worshiper.

If anyone loves the world in that way, the love of the Father is not in that person. This reminds me of the difficulty many of us have with the thought, "How close *can* I get to sin without sinning?" How many porn websites, how many clothes taken off, how much can I pilfer from the office, how can I fudge on my taxes, et cetera, and not actually step over the line into sin? "If anyone loves the world, the love of the Father is not in that person." I think God would say to any of us tempted to give in when in those situations, "Instead, why don't you stay as close to *Me* as you can, rather than seeing how far away you can get? With all you receive from Me, this world has nothing to offer you."

"For all that is in the world is not from the Father but is from the world." And God boils down everything into 3 easy categories:

- the lust/desires of the flesh
- the lust/desires of the eyes
- the pride of life

These were the things that Satan used against Jesus in Matthew 4 and Luke 4 after the Lord's 40 days in the wilderness alone. By the way, those were not the only temptations Jesus faced on earth. Every moment of His earthly life, He was faced with temptation to turn from God and trust His own understanding. That's how Hebrews 4:15 can truthfully say, "He was tempted in *every* way as we are, and yet was without sin."

The world's system, directed by the one given temporary authority over it (Satan), tries to drag us away from God by what appeals to our flesh – sensuality, sex, drugs, money. And by what appeals to our eyes – those previous things, plus appearance, physical beauty and emphasis on comparison with others. And also, by the pride of life – status, recognition, importance, significance. All of that is from the world and is not from God the Father. The things of the world stand in direct opposition to God and God's design of love – loving Him and loving others. And God says clearly here that those things and all that goes with them, and the world itself, are passing away. So, to love the world and the things in the world is worthless – it will not last and will not – *cannot* – deliver what it promises.

But whoever does the will of God abides forever. Once again, doing the will of God is easily shown to be an impossibility by human beings trying to do it on their own. But Jesus Christ Himself always did the will of the Father – and He always *will* do the Father's will. He is the only one who can. That is how God can make that promise to us, "…whoever does the will of the Father abides forever." It is *Him* who does it.

I know this chapter is getting long, but I hope you're experiencing what the title promised – you don't want it to end! Two more passages to build our faith and show us the power of God's plan.

Born of God

1 John 2:28,29:

> And now, little children, abide in Him, so that when He appears we may have confidence and not shrink from Him in shame at His coming. If you know that He is righteous, you may be sure that everyone who practices righteousness has been born of Him.

"Abide" is a key word in 1 John – it appears many times. Your Bible translation may use the synonym "dwell." Here, we are given the command to abide in Him: not abide around Him or near Him; not to abide in our efforts to be like Him. We are commanded to abide *in Him*, so that when He appears (whether that means His coming at the end or when we close our eyes on this earthly life and He is the next thing we see), we may have confidence and not shrink back from Him in shame.

Does anyone reading this have *that* concern? How am I going to explain those stupid decisions or actions? Can He/Does He really forgive me? God knew what He was getting into when He rescued us. We have already mentioned 1 John 2:2 – "…if anyone does sin, we have an Advocate with the Father, Jesus Christ the righteous." And also, Romans 8:1, "There is therefore now no condemnation for those who are in Christ." We can come to God confidently because of God's own work through Christ. And even if we *do* sin, it is still God's work through Christ that allows us to come with confidence and without shame.

First John 2:28,29 assures believers that we *can* stand confidently, not shrinking back from our failures, when we abide in Him. Abiding in Him implies clearly that He abides in us — Him, living His life in us. If you know that He is righteous, you may be sure that everyone who practices righteousness like He does has been born of Him. It is *His* righteousness being seen, not mankind's. It is *Him* being seen. It is *Him* we trust in and rely on.

> Since we have confidence to enter the holy places by the blood of Jesus, by the new and living way that He opened for us through the curtain, that is, through His flesh…let us draw near with a true heart in full assurance of faith…let us hold fast the confession of our hope without wavering…

let us consider how to stir up one another to love and good works...encouraging one another, and all the more as you see the Day drawing near. (Hebrews 10:19-25)

We can do all of that because it is *Him* living in *us*.

Obviously, 1 John has a lot more to say, and this is a full and rich little book. All five chapters are important and meaningful and vital – I highly encourage all followers of Jesus to spend much time studying and learning and hearing from God through 1 John. We have looked at a few passages that throw people for a loop sometimes. Here's the last one.

Cannot Keep On

"Everyone who makes a practice of sinning also practices lawlessness: sin is lawlessness. You know that He appeared in order **to take away sins**, and **in Him** there is no sin. **No one who abides in Him keeps on sinning**; no one who keeps on sinning has either seen Him or known Him. Little children, let no one deceive you. Whoever practices righteousness is righteous, **as He is righteous**. Whoever makes a practice of sinning is of the devil, for the devil has been sinning from the beginning. The reason the Son of God appeared was to destroy the works of the devil. No one born of God makes a practice of sinning, for God's seed abides in him; and **he cannot keep on sinning**, because **he has been born of God**. By this it is evident who are the children of God, and who are the children of the devil: whoever does

not practice righteousness is not of God, nor is the
one who does not love his brother." (1 John 3:4-10)

BOOM! Those verses either rip you to shreds or they crank you
up with excitement! Clearly, God's expectation of His people –
believers, followers of Jesus Christ – is to have zero contact with sin.
In no way can we get the idea that a little bit of sin in His people is
okay with God. Jesus Christ came to take away sins (v 5). And the
very next phrase means something – "in Him there is NO sin." He
came to take away sin and *in Him* there is no sin. IN HIM. That
kind of life is God's desire for everyone. When a person is *in* Christ,
GOD says, there is no sin. Verse 6, no one who abides in Christ
keeps on sinning. Sin is not – cannot – possibly be a consistent and
regular feature of the life of someone who abides *IN* Christ.

How can that be? This scares me, because I still sin.

It is *Him* living *His* sinless life *in* those who believe. Not them
working really hard to avoid sin and gut it out. Christ *in* you, the
hope of glory! And what a glorious thing to see the righteousness
of God demonstrated through one's life. What an incredible
realization that Jesus Christ *is* alive, and He is showing Himself
in *me* for His glory by His power.

If you experience sin regularly and consistently in your life, *listen!*
DON'T GIVE UP! You're at a huge decision point. Instead of
giving up, realize that you are not *in* Christ. You are trying to live
a Christian life without the power of the only one who *can* live it.
No wonder life is disappointing and frustrating! And what's the
answer? Same as always – repent and believe. Turn from trying by
your own effort to produce the life of Christ and trust Him to do
it. As Major Thomas often said, "You cannot do it. He never said
you could. But He *can* do it. He always said He would."

Verse 7, "Little children, let no one deceive you." This point is a major target of Satan, the enemy of our souls. Satan does not want followers of Jesus to know this or live this way. But do not be deceived. Whoever practices righteousness – lives a life of consistent and active righteousness – *is* righteous, and here it is again, as *He* is righteous. It is God's righteousness being seen in a person who lives in righteousness. Just like whoever makes a practice of sinning is of the devil. It is the character of the devil himself being seen in that person. That's who the devil is and always has been since he trusted himself instead of God.

Jesus came to destroy the works of the devil. Think about that one. The works of the devil – the lust of the flesh, the lust of the eyes, and the pride of life – are nothing like the Father. Those are the things of the world which is passing away (1 John 2:15-17). Jesus came to destroy those things – not just in the world, but in the lives of His people who have to exist in the world until evacuated by death or by His coming. So, not only did Jesus come to bring mankind forgiveness of sins, reinstatement of life and light, restoration to God's design for mankind, but He also came to destroy the things that drag us away *from* that life. In order for you and me to experience the life God offers, He Himself had to remove the barriers. Jesus on earth had the barriers in His face daily, as we do now. But the work of Jesus Christ allows His followers to be undisturbed by the devil's schemes and to defeat them (as it says in Ephesians 6 – by *God's* armor). And by trusting Jesus Christ alone and keeping our eyes on Him, the Author and Finisher of our faith, it is now possible to see His life in us, through us, around us.

Seed of God in Believers

The final verses of this passage are extremely graphic and can easily get people off track. So, be careful. Hear what is being said and how it has dramatic and God-sized impact on us who believe.

Verse 9, "No one born of God makes a practice of sinning, for God's seed abides in him; and he cannot keep sinning, because he has been born of God." Take a moment and remember Luke chapter 2. A young virgin named Mary was visited by Gabriel, an angel of God, and told that she would conceive a child by the work of the Spirit of God. Since the Father of Jesus was sinless, Jesus was sinless. Verse 9 clearly says that no one who is born of God makes a practice of sinning, because God's seed abides in that person.

This is the graphic part – keep your wits about you, don't get distracted and DON'T allow the enemy a foothold. The Greek word here for "seed" is "*sperma*." I do not think it is a mistake on God's part to choose *that* word to describe what it is that keeps those who are born of Him from practicing sin. God uses the *same thing* that kept Jesus from sinning to keep *us* from sinning. But wait! None of us were conceived by the Spirit or born of a virgin. So, how can God say this and how can it be true?

God can say this, and it *is* true, because *Jesus Christ* lives *in* believers. *He* was conceived as a human being without sin and He lives in human lives without sin because His Father is God. The same sinlessness that happened in Jesus Christ is now available to us as He lives in us. It is *Him in us*.

We will close this chapter there. We didn't even mention 1 John 4:17, "…as He is, so are we in this world." But, those were just a few passages in the short little book of 1 John. There are more passages to look at and gain insight on what God has made possible for human beings through Jesus Christ. Even though this chapter is ending, there's more to thrill our souls – and there are huge questions to answer. Keep reading!

CHAPTER 5
More Truth to Celebrate!

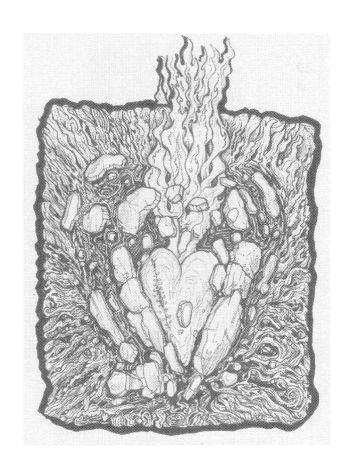

I know that some are reading and getting more and more frustrated.

HOW? Why doesn't it work for me? You're making me feel like I don't have enough faith to live this way.

As we look at passages in this chapter, I want to help with some of those questions. Chapter 6 specifically addresses those questions. Don't give up – Christ in you is the plan and purpose of God for every person who believes.

Jesus and the Father

In chapters 13 through 17 of his gospel account, John records things Jesus said to the Twelve in the Upper Room on the last night of His earthly life. Jesus knew His death was coming, and the things He told these men are incredibly important – no one talks about things that don't matter knowing the end is coming. Philip, one of the Twelve, makes a request:

> Philip said to Him, 'Lord, show us the Father, and it is enough for us.' Jesus said to him, 'Have I been with you so long, and you still do not know Me, Philip? Whoever has seen Me has seen the Father. How can you say, 'Show us the Father?' Do you not believe that **I am in the Father** and **the Father is in Me**? The words I say to you I do not speak on My own authority, but the Father who dwells in Me does His works. Believe Me that I am in the Father and the Father is in Me, or else believe on account of the works themselves. Truly, truly, I say to you, whoever believes in Me **will also do the works that I do**, and **greater works than these will he do**, because I am going to the

Father. Whatever you ask **in My name**, this I will
do, **that the Father may be glorified** in the Son.
If you ask Me anything **in My name**, I will do it.
(John 14:8-14)

Somehow Philip, and probably the rest of the Twelve, had missed
something vital in Jesus's teachings while He was with them: "I
am in the Father and the Father is in Me." Before we go on, what is
the theme of this book? Christ living His life IN you. This sounds
very much like what Jesus is reminding Philip of here.

And as Jesus lived His life *in* the Father, it led to certain realities.
One, He brings up here in this passage. "The words I say to you I
do not speak on My own authority, but the Father who dwells in
Me does His works." We could quote a number of passages where
Jesus says this same kind of thing – what I do is really the Father
doing it – what I am saying is really the Father saying it – I can do
nothing except what I see the Father do.

This is *REALLY* important! *Jesus lived the way He calls us to live.*
He depended totally on the Father to make it through human life
the way God intended human life to be. He calls *us* to depend
totally on Him to make it through human life the way God intends
human life to be. The Father dwelt in Jesus (and we could make a
really strong case that the Father dwelt in Jesus through the Spirit).
Jesus dwells in believers through the Spirit. As an advertisement
for a store in Omaha called "The ½ Price Store" used to say, "IT'S
THE SAME THING!" The Father in Him – Him in us through
the Spirit.

Greater Works Than Jesus

This reality opens the door that allows Jesus to say that the one
who believes in Him will do greater works than He did. If Jesus

is telling the truth that He does nothing except what He sees the Father do – and He *is* telling the truth, the truth is who He *is*, John 14:6 – then when Jesus healed someone, or Jesus calmed a storm, or Jesus walked on water, *who* did those things? *Not* Jesus – the *Father.* The Lord Jesus emptied Himself fully of His God abilities, (Philippians 2:7), and came to live life on earth fully as a human being. He was and still is God. His character did not change. But He laid aside everything temporarily so that He could show us how human life was meant to be lived. I often use this example for our church family: I am a guitar player (not that great, but able to play most anything sufficiently). If someone walked in the door of our church building after I had put my guitar down and I was preaching, the person who came in would have no idea that I was a guitar player. I had laid aside my guitar-playing abilities temporarily. It did not and does not change my ability to play the guitar or the fact that I am a guitar player, but at that time, I laid it aside. This is what Jesus did in becoming a human being.

So, with that in mind, when Jesus healed or did some miracle or raised someone from the dead, Him having emptied Himself was still in place. He did not pull out His God powers to do *anything* while on earth as a human being. He did everything He did *as* a human being fully submitted to the Father, who is the one who did *His* works. That opens *another* door.

If the Father did the Father's work through a submitted Jesus Christ when He lived a human life on earth, and Jesus says that we will do greater works than those, we can now see *how* that can happen! It is Jesus Christ doing Jesus Christ's work through submitted followers of Jesus Christ living *real* human lives on earth.

Jesus says in John 14:12 that whoever believes in Him will do the works He does and greater works than He did *because* He is going to the Father. Elsewhere, in John 14 through 16, Jesus tells His followers (including us) of the coming of the indwelling Spirit of God in our lives. And Jesus says that it would be better that He went away. It would be to our advantage because, rather than Jesus being here on earth in one place as a human being, He can now, through the indwelling Spirit, be in every believer all the time (John 16:7). Jesus will continue to do His works in His people. This happens through the indwelling Spirit at work in submitted followers who trust Him as He trusted the Father. Jesus could do only certain things in His limited time and location on earth, although the Father even reached across geographic space to show Himself through the Lord Jesus. Now, living His life in millions at the same time, He can, will, and does the same kinds of things He did when He was here and greater things.

Not About Miracles

Let me say here, this book is *not* about us doing miracles. This book is not about *us*! This book is about Jesus Christ *being* Jesus Christ in the lives of His people who trust Him and follow Him. In the same way Jesus allowed God the Father to *be* God the Father through His life, He has made it possible to be Himself through our lives. I would not expect that suddenly you or I will be able to heal people, or raise people from the dead, or any other miraculous thing. But neither am I saying that God will not or does not do those things. He certainly *does*. If a human being lives in submission to Jesus Christ, and Jesus Christ requires someone to reach out and touch a dead person or a sick person, Jesus Christ can do that. He does not need my permission or anyone else's. He is God. He can do what He wants.

The apostles, in the early days of the Church in the book of Acts, went around doing "signs and wonders." But remember who is the subject of the book of Acts. Your Bible might have the title,

"The Acts of the Apostles." Sorry, that is incorrect. It should read, "The Acts of the Holy Spirit." When the Spirit came and moved in to human lives starting in Acts 2, He opened up a world of opportunities for God to be seen in and through the lives of ordinary people. That is still true today. So, I am not saying, "Go out and do miracles." If miracles become the focus, we have, once again, developed an idol worship problem. I *am* saying, "Go out and allow Jesus Christ to live His life in you in every circumstance." Who knows what will happen! God does, of course! And He will be the one we celebrate and glorify and exalt when He does His stuff.

Image Bearers of God

Because Jesus went to the Father, He now has the tremendous advantage of being not only omnipresent Himself, but of being many places on earth *in believers* at the same time, showing Himself through them. This thought connects to another part of Scripture — the beginning of Scripture.

> So, God created man in His own image, in the image of God He created him, male and female He created them. (Genesis 1:27)

One reason God created the universe and the earth and mankind was to show Himself. In fact, He created mankind in His own image, with characteristics and character qualities that show Him, so that *He* would be seen. Of course, Genesis 3 happened, mankind sinned and went our own way, away from God's design. But God's design is still what God wants, as we saw in Chapter 3 of this book. Now, through Jesus Christ living the Father's life through the indwelling Spirit of God in human beings, the ability to bear God's image has been reinstated in mankind. And we do not have to *try* to look like God – He can look like Himself *in* us as we are submitted to Him.

Back to John 14. Jesus says that whatever believers ask in His name, He will do, so that the *Father* may be glorified in the Son. This statement comes immediately after the promise that believers will do the works Jesus did and even greater works.

What does it mean to ask "in Jesus' name?" Are those the magic words we tack on the end of our prayers? Are they mystical in some other way?

No. To ask "in Jesus' name" has an extremely significant purpose and implication. And that purpose and implication is the reason for Jesus saying that *whatever* we ask in His name, He will do. It is the phrase at the end of that statement that defines what "in Jesus' name" means: "That the Father may be glorified in the Son." When you or I ask, "in Jesus' name," we are asking for Jesus to do things that will glorify the Father as Jesus does those things.

How do I know what will glorify the Father through the Son? How can I make sure that I'm not asking for things that make *me* happy or make *me* look good? Here's where the rubber meets the road and will get us to the next chapter when we look specifically at questions and issues that cause people to be discouraged and disappointed.

How do I know what glorifies the Father through the Son?

Because I know the Father and the Son.

Let's look at what is sometimes called "The High Priestly Prayer" of Jesus in John 17. In this prayer on the eve of His crucifixion, He prays for Himself, for His disciples who lived and walked with

Him, and for *us*, who now believe because of what the original disciples said about Him (17:20). To know what glorifies the Father through the Son is to know God in His fullness.

> When Jesus had spoken these words [chapters 13 – 16 in the Upper Room], He lifted up His eyes to heaven, and said, "Father, the hour has come, glorify Your Son **that the Son may glorify You**, since You have given Him authority over all flesh, to give eternal life to all whom You have given Him. And this is eternal life, **that they may know You**, the only true God, **and Jesus Christ whom You have sent**." (John 17:1-3)

Jesus asks God the Father to glorify Him, the Son of God, so that the Son may glorify the Father. What was about to happen? The betrayal, kangaroo court, persecution, humiliation, scourging, ridicule, slander, rejection, exhaustion, and finally, the gruesome execution of Jesus Christ. God – whether the Father in heaven, or Jesus and the Spirit on earth, having come from heaven – God *knew* what was about to happen. Jesus *knew* what was about to happen. He saw it before He ever emptied Himself and came to earth to live a human life. And He refers to this as something that will glorify the Father.

In that list of upcoming suffering just listed, we did not include the end of the story – the resurrection. Nor did we include the coming of the Spirit Helper (see Chapter 6). But as Jesus readied Himself for suffering, He prayed that God the Father would be glorified by what happened to God the Son. *We* look at what happened to God the Son, and we don't see much that is glorious. This is a great reminder to us of a principle that we must deal with as we anticipate experiencing the life of Christ in us. The principle is found clearly in 1 Corinthians 1. I will summarize: God does things almost completely opposite of how we would do things.

God was preparing to use suffering to glorify Himself – Father, Son, Spirit. Suffering. We wouldn't plan things that way. But the suffering of Jesus Christ is what Jesus was praying for the Father to use to glorify Himself (Jesus), and for the Son's suffering to glorify the Father.

Hebrews 12 speaks of how Jesus could look this way at the suffering He would go through:

> Therefore, since we are surrounded by so great a cloud of witnesses (the faithful people spoken of in chapter 11), let us also lay aside every weight, and sin which clings so closely, and let us run with endurance the race that is set before us, looking to Jesus, the founder and perfecter of our faith, who **for the joy that was set before Him** endured the cross, despising the shame, and is seated at the right hand of the throne of God. (Hebrews 12:1,2)

The joy that was set before Jesus as He prayed and anticipated the terrible events He was about to suffer, was His Father being glorified because of it. Included in that glory and joy was also the knowledge that millions of people, including you and me, would be rescued from sin and death by faith *in* His death and resurrection – which brings glory to the Father. And also, that those same millions of people would be able to experience the righteousness of God in them through Jesus Christ's life through the indwelling Spirit, bringing glory to the Father.

But the glory He anticipated came through suffering. Is that how you and I view glory? If we knew what was coming, suffering-wise, would we pray for God to be glorified through it? *This way of thinking must become our way of thinking.*

Transformed

> I appeal to you therefore, brothers, by the mercies of God, to present your bodies as a living sacrifice, holy and acceptable to God, which is your spiritual worship. Do not be conformed to this world, but be **transformed by the renewal of your mind**, that by testing you may discern what is the will of God, what is good and acceptable and perfect. (Romans 12:1,2)

Those words, "spiritual worship," could very easily be translated "logical response." "Present your bodies as a living sacrifice, which is your logical response to the mercies of God." The Greek word translated "spiritual" in the ESV is "*logikos*." I have asked Greek scholars and those who understand Greek why the translators in most English versions did not use the most obvious English word to translate *logikos* – "logical." No one has given me an explanation, except that it *might* mean "spiritual" or some of the other ways it is translated. My pea-brain says, Go with what is obvious – and logical!

It doesn't matter if you have been a believer for a long time or you just got saved reading Chapter 3 – although new believers don't have as much baggage – but over the years, we have been taught (in any branch of Christianity of which we have been a part) to be able to explain and understand everything about God. In fact, when I got saved, in the mid-1970s, there had been a theological war raging for over 50 years about the role of the Spirit in the lives of believers. Denominations had been formed to avoid overemphasizing the role of the Spirit. I was actually taught that

God no longer did miracles. It took me years to hear from the Spirit of God that God can do whatever He wants, and He does not need my permission or the permission of theologians or Bible college teachers. This is not to denigrate them – they, too, were products of their teaching, and seeking to be fully devoted to Jesus Christ as much they knew how. They were just unintentionally off-base.

But now, as followers of Jesus, we must be transformed – metamorphized – changed – by the renewing of our minds. And we can trust God to do that because of His mercy, laid out clearly by Paul in chapters 1 through 11 in Romans. I am writing this book to encourage anyone to whom the Spirit of God is speaking, to re-examine what it means to live a so-called Christian life. I am writing to encourage anyone to whom the Spirit is speaking, to allow God to transform him or her as He renews his or her mind. In God's view (the *correct* view, by the way), suffering leads to glory. Weakness produces strength. Foolishness (in the world's eyes) leads to wisdom (in God's eyes).

For you and me to know God the Father and Jesus Christ whom He sent, we need major mind-renewal *from* God leading to transformation. Jesus prayed for the glory of the Father through His suffering. Do you understand the suffering of Jesus? As you have considered and are reflecting on His suffering, are you getting to know Him better? Have you spent time thinking through everything that happened to Him – not just the day He died, but every day of His earthly life? To know Him in His sufferings leads to deeper love *of* Him. The apostle Paul makes a tremendous case for this in Philippians 3. He warns his Gentile (non-Jewish) readers about those (Jewish supposed-Christians) who "mutilate the flesh" by requiring circumcision of non-Jewish people in order to become followers of Jesus. This is a works-based salvation. As he makes his case, Paul reminds his readers that if being Jewish was a requirement for being a follower of Jesus, then Paul himself would be the poster-child for that kind of Christianity. But that's not at all what it takes.

> If anyone else thinks he has reason for confidence in the flesh, I have more: circumcised on the eighth day, of the people of Israel, of the tribe of Benjamin, a Hebrew of Hebrews; as to the law, a Pharisee; as to zeal, a persecutor of the church; as to righteousness under the law, blameless. But, whatever gain I had, I counted as loss for the sake of Christ. Indeed, I count everything as loss because of the **surpassing worth of knowing Christ Jesus my Lord**. For His sake I have suffered the loss of all things and count them as rubbish, in order that I may gain Christ and be found **in Him**, not having a righteousness of my own that comes from the law, but that which comes through faith **in Christ, the righteousness from God that depends on faith** – that I may know Him and **the power of His resurrection**, and **may share His sufferings**, becoming **like Him in His death**, that by any means possible I may attain the resurrection from the dead. (Philippians 3:4b-11)

Jesus prayed for the Father to be glorified in His suffering. Paul sought to know Jesus his Lord, viewing everything else in his life as rubbish compared to knowing Jesus. And knowing Jesus, as Paul makes his case, includes sharing in His sufferings.

This goes against most everything we have been taught to believe, especially us Americans. But God sees things correctly, and He says here that His glory comes through suffering. Until you and I can believe God and agree with Him and seek His glory joyfully like Jesus did (and I don't think our suffering will be anywhere near as intense as His), we are still in need of the transforming work of God to renew our minds on the issue.

Knowing God and knowing Jesus is eternal life. Knowing God and knowing Jesus allows us to trust Him in every situation regardless of our view of the situation. Jesus lived that way, trusting the Father. Go back to John 17.

> I do not ask for these only [His disciples who walked with Him], but also for those who will believe in Me [us] through their word [which we now know as the New Testament], that they may all be one, just as You, Father, are in Me, and I in You, that they also may be in Us, so that the world may believe that You have sent Me. The glory that You have given Me I have given them, that they may be one even as We are one, **I in them** and **You in Me**, that they may become perfectly one, so that the world may know that You sent Me and loved them even as You have loved Me. (John 17:20-23)

The way Jesus lived His earthly life is the way He asks God the Father to allow *us* to live earthly life: us in Christ in the same exact way as Christ was in the Father. Remember what Jesus said, "I do nothing unless I see the Father do it." "I say nothing unless I hear the Father say it." Jesus prays for the Father to make *us* one with *Him* just as *He* was one with the *Father*. The Father lived the Father's life in the Lord Jesus through the indwelling Spirit. Jesus desires to live Jesus's life in us through the indwelling Spirit.

Did you know that about yourself, believer? Did you know that *that* is what Jesus desires? Do you know Jesus in such a way that you can trust Him in any and all situations, to show Himself through you as you give up living your own life and allow Him to live His?

You may have just answered "no" to all of those questions. That's OK. Life is a process, and you're *in* the process. But are you seeing that this is God's plan? Do you *want* to experience life the way God intended life to be lived? He can do what He does in *you* – there's no doubt about that. He is doing it in *me* – and I know who I am! He did it in Paul – Saul of Tarsus, at the time – when he was a persecutor of the church and participant in the murder of at least one follower of Jesus. He did it in Peter, who denied even knowing Jesus three times. He did it in His brothers James and Jude, who ridiculed Him and did not believe in Him until after His resurrection. He did it in Mary from the town of Magdala – a demon-possessed prostitute. In order to believe and take God at His Word, it takes His work of transformation as we review what we *think* we know. We do not need to excuse or soften or dismiss anything God says. We are called to trust Him and do what He says.

Paul records his prayer for the believers in Philippi in *Philippians 1:9-11.*

> And it is my prayer **that your love may abound** more and more, **with knowledge and all discernment**, so that you may approve what is excellent, and so be pure and blameless for the day of Christ, **filled with the fruit of righteousness that comes through Jesus Christ to the glory and praise of God.**

Paul prays for these believers that their love would grow in knowledge and all discernment. In knowledge of *what*? In all discernment of *what*? In knowledge and all discernment of what is excellent, leading to purity and blamelessness, allowing them to be filled with the fruit of righteousness that comes *through Jesus Christ* to the glory and praise of God. Paul prayed that people would love more and more, knowing and discerning the best things – God's things – and that knowing and discerning those things would lead to God's righteousness showing in them through the work of Jesus Christ. The answer to Paul's prayer was Jesus Christ *in* them, being Himself.

Go back to the Bible and read the lives of these people and see how the Lord transformed them, how their minds were renewed, and who they became by *His* power at work in them. The world will know – or at least have to think about – who Jesus is and what He can do in human lives if the world sees *Him in us*. Knowing God the Father, knowing Jesus Christ whom He sent, and experiencing the righteousness of God through the indwelling Spirit – God in His fullness – allows those who follow Jesus to see Christ *in* us. It is *Him*.

CHAPTER 6
Questions/Concerns

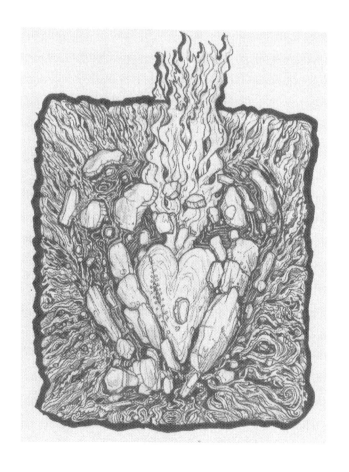

So, let's get to the things that have been percolating in you as we have presented the Christian life as Jesus living *His* life in believers. These may be arguments or questions, doubts or disagreements. I would like to handle the most prevalent ones in this chapter, and, as you know, I have addressed a few as we have gone through.

We'll address four questions or concerns you may have – or that might summarize most of the issues.

1. I have TRIED, but it just doesn't happen. Either I don't have enough faith or you're wrong, Mike.

I assume when a person says, "I have *tried*," they mean, "I have sought to give my life completely to Jesus and deny myself, but I don't see Him showing up through me." If that is your case, I have hope for you. But if you're saying, "I have *tried*," and you mean "I have put all kinds of effort into being what I think a Christian is supposed to be, but I am still the same person I always was," then, like the Bob Newhart clip – "STOP IT!" Stop *trying* to live a life you *cannot* live. Only Jesus can live His life. You can't, so don't try. He can. You don't have to try. Let Him be Himself in you. Re-read Chapters 5 and 6, review and revisit how you were taught the Christian life and determine what does not line up with how Jesus describes it. Then repent and believe – turn from your own understanding and ways and trust Him and His understanding (Proverbs 3:5,6).

For those who are saying, "I have sought to give my life completely to Jesus and deny myself, but I don't see Him showing up through me," let's address what might be keeping you from experiencing the life of Christ in you.

First, remember that the life of Christ in you is not something you *do*. It is not some action you take or some program you follow that produces results. Christ in you happens as you *know* Jesus. How did you get to know your parents or your spouse or your children? You weren't enrolled in some kind of program or school course. You did not follow a checklist of items to put into practice. You spent time with them – whether it was intentional or not. Babies are not intentionally involved in getting to know their parents – and parents are not going through some step-by-step process to get to know their children. The natural process of spending time together results in knowing one another. Time spent with the one/ ones we love leads to knowledge of them and love.

God has given us several ways to know Him. His Word, the Bible, is a primary way. From Genesis 1:1 through Revelation 22:21, God has given us everything we need to know Him and to know His love for us. The Bible is, from cover to cover, the story of God who wants us to know Him, to show Him, to experience Him, to be with Him, to come back to Him, and to join Him forever. When we read the Bible, we can read it with *that* understanding and expectation. Every page – every list of names we can't pronounce – every location in the Promised Land where something happened – every instruction and doctrinal truth – *everything* is there for us to know God the Father and Jesus Christ whom He sent. We can use step-by-step methods in Bible reading, that's okay, but our mindset must be that we are seeking and getting to know the one who did everything necessary to bring us to Himself.

The Lord has also given us the indwelling Spirit as another way to teach us and lead us to know Jesus Christ and God the Father. In John 16, the Lord Jesus calls the Spirit of God our Helper. He helps us know Jesus. He helps us know the Father. Just a little tangent here – someone else is referred to as a "helper" in the Scripture: the woman whom God made for Adam – Eve – and truthfully, all wives. "It is not good that the man should be alone. I will make him a helper who is like him." Have you ever considered this - what did Adam need help with? He was the perfect specimen of a human being. He had no house, he lived in perfect conditions in a perfect garden – he didn't need someone to do the housework. He had no clothes – he didn't need someone to do laundry. He had no children at the beginning – he didn't need someone to watch the kids. He could eat of all but one tree in the Garden of Eden – he didn't need someone to cook for him. What did that guy possibly need help with?

God gave Eve to Adam as a helper so that Adam would be the kind of man God wanted him to be. Genesis 1:27 – "in the image of God He created him (mankind), male and female He created them." In order for mankind to show who God is, male and female were both necessary. For Adam to be what God intended mankind to be, Adam needed Eve.

Jesus calls the Spirit, who comes to indwell believers, the Helper. We need a lot of help, obviously, but God sent the Spirit as our Helper to help us be what God intends us to be. Eve was initially a picture of the Spirit of God – later she, along with Adam, blew it. And as we seek to know the Father and Jesus Christ whom He sent, the Spirit helps us by bringing to our minds everything Jesus said, by teaching us what the Scripture means, by sustaining us in trouble.

God has also given us the Church – other followers of Jesus – as a way to help us know Him. Hopefully this book, written by me, another follower of Jesus, will help you to experience and know Jesus Christ living in you. Hopefully in your local church, and in a small group you're in or some other kind of fellowship group, there are people who know Jesus and can share with you not merely *how* they came to know Jesus, but who will spend life with you knowing Him. This is called discipleship, doing life together; loving, learning, and following Jesus. In conjunction with His

Word and His Spirit, God uses His people to help His people know Him.

My encouragement to you if you've tried and it hasn't worked, is to try again, but this time, realizing that it is Christ living His own life. Allow the God of all knowledge to work in you to know Him as He is so that you can trust Him and do what He says. Allow the God of resurrection to bring your mortal body to life and transform you through the renewing of your mind. Allow Him to take what you have always believed and tear it apart and rebuild it with what is true. Allow the God of Adam and Noah and Abraham and Moses and David, the God of Peter, James, and John, the God of Paul and Silas and Timothy to use His people to walk side by side with you, learning to know Him together.

2. Are you saying that if God expects our lives to be like the life of Jesus, we will be able to do miracles like He did? I don't believe that.

First, let me remind all of us, this book is not about us doing miracles. If you have read between the lines, I don't even think *Jesus* did miracles, in the way we think of it. It is pretty clear to me that He did what the Father led Him to do – to believe the Father to live the Father's life in Jesus. And the Father did the miracles. If God wants to heal someone or raise someone from the dead or replace a missing limb, He can do that. There is nothing too difficult for Him. If He wants a human being involved in that process, He can use a human being. Do I think we will all be out there doing miracles? No. But I think God has been patiently waiting for His people to get out of the way and let God *BE* God in us, whatever the results.

Second, this is a Romans 12:1,2 issue. If Jesus said in John 14 that whoever believes in Him will do the works He did and will do greater works, then, as a follower of Jesus and believer in God,

I have to set aside my understanding of the natural world and believe God to be God. Remember when Jesus sent the disciples across the Sea of Galilee on the boat and He later came walking up to the boat *on* the water? What happened next? Peter, believing in Jesus Christ alone, called out to the Lord and the Lord told Peter to jump out and walk over *to* Him. And Peter *did*. Peter walked on water. Peter was just a guy. He was a hothead and he often spoke before thinking. He was a guy like you are a guy (unless you're a gal, but it still follows). *Peter walked on water.* At least until his human understanding went back into action – then he sank. Reality is that no matter what mankind says about the laws of nature, God, the Creator of nature, can do whatever He wants with whomever He wants in any way He wants.

As a Romans 12:1,2 issue, I must set aside what *seems* to be the truth and trust in the one who *is* the truth. Truth is exactly what God says it is, not what mankind says. Sometimes mankind stumbles into agreement with God. But when God states something different, *He* is the one to be believed and trusted. *He* is the one who has it right.

So, will you or I do miracles? No. If anything miraculous happens around you or me, just like with Jesus, it is God the Father who does it and God the Father who should be glorified and acknowledged. And remember, seeking for miracles to happen because of the obvious thrill, instead of seeking the Lord, is idol worship. Miracles are the wrong focus. Jesus Christ alone is to be our focus.

3. Because of the way Jesus became a human being, He had a great advantage over us. He had no sin nature to deal with. We do. It is not possible for us to live like He lived.

I love this concern because the answer is so exciting! Once again, Romans 12:1 & 2-thinking helps us – transformation by the renewing of our minds.

Adam, the first man, and Jesus were extremely similar. Adam was made of dust and God breathed life into Adam. Jesus was conceived in the body of a woman who was made of dust – and we see that He became flesh made of dust like the rest of humanity. His Father was perfect and sinless. But so also was Adam's Father perfect and sinless. Everyone else's fathers are sinful and broken because of what Adam became. But Adam's Father formed him and breathed life into him and Adam became a living soul. There was no sin in the creation or construction or nature of Adam, same as Jesus.

Adam and Jesus were put to the same test: believe God and live, or trust self and die. Adam failed, even though he did not have a sinful nature, just like Jesus. Jesus did not fail. He remained in the state God always desired mankind to be, fully dependent on the Father. Jesus was tempted in every way as we are, yet without sin (Hebrews 4:15). Adam failed the first test he encountered. Jesus passed every test He encountered. Was it because He did not have a sin nature?

Major Ian Thomas made an insightful statement to consider: If some person had asked the Lord Jesus how He made it through life without sinning, He would *not* have answered, "It's because I'm God." He would have answered, "It's because I am MAN! I am Man the way God intended man to be." Adam had the same opportunity – maybe *better.* He had no sin nature, perfect conditions, only one woman in his thoughts. The Lord Jesus lived under much worse conditions than Adam. He had the same nature – without sin – but was surrounded by sin and sinful human beings for His entire earthly life. He had temptations and distractions galore – sexual and otherwise. And Jesus, having emptied Himself of His God abilities and taken on the form of mankind ("living in flesh," Philippians 2), lived just as God desired mankind to live. Jesus *was* what Adam failed to be – a *real* human being.

So, was it *easy* for the Lord Jesus to reject sin simply because He did not have a sin nature? Well, was it easy for Adam? No. Adam gave in on the first test. Jesus lived fully dependent upon the Father for everything. We have looked at how He described His earthly life. Did His lack of a sin nature make it easier for Him to rely on the Father? Did it for Adam? No. Both were put in the same situation, but only Jesus lived how God designed and desired.

Well, if it was not being sin nature-free, what *was* it that allowed the Lord Jesus to live the way He did? Read this carefully – it is vital: Adam, upon creation, knew nothing except God and what God revealed to him. He did not even know there *was* good or evil or a difference between them – not until he ate the fruit of the tree of the knowledge of good and evil. But when Satan, through the serpent, came to Adam and claimed that God was lying to him, Adam believed Satan. Adam would have believed anyone. Adam did not have a concept of good or evil at the time. BUT! Adam *did* know what God had said. "Do not eat the fruit of that tree because if you eat it, you will die." Adam likely did not even know what "die" meant – there was no death. But regardless, Adam knew what God said and he did precisely what God told him *not* to do anyway. It did not matter what Satan said. Adam could have responded, "I like you, serpent, but God said, 'Don't eat that fruit,' so I will trust and believe God." Unfortunately, Adam didn't say that.

Instead, Adam, existing without a sin nature, took the word of someone other than God and acted on it. He stepped away from trusting God, and instead trusted not just Satan, but Adam's own understanding, which was very limited. And sin worked in Adam, and that led to the ruin of Adam and of mankind. Notice, Adam did not *need* a sin nature to commit sin. His flesh responded to sin when he was presented with sin.

The thing that allowed Jesus Christ to live on earth as a human being free from sin was *His knowledge of and dependence on the Father.* It could not have been His lack of a sin nature – Adam lacked a sin nature, but he sinned. The flesh of the Lord Jesus was faced with the same temptations and restrictions as Adam and as us. His flesh would have been subject to the draw of sin. But His relationship with the Father kept Him from giving in. His sin-free life shows *us* the overwhelming and incredible power of the knowledge of God in the life of a human being.

Perhaps the *flesh* of Jesus was different than yours and mine and Adam's, and that's how He could live without sin. Did the conception of the Lord Jesus by the Spirit of God result in His flesh being incorruptible and unassailable – different from ours? We know His blood was incorruptible – did that transfer into His flesh? Before we look at the Bible, let's review a few facts we know:

- the Lord Jesus aged
- the Lord Jesus experienced hunger and thirst (and without being irreverent, the natural results of eating and drinking happened to Him, too)
- dirt clung to His feet like everyone else's
- emotion was part of His life – He wept, He got angry, He had compassion
- during His final hours, when He was whipped, He was torn and He bled, and when He was nailed to the cross, He bled and eventually suffocated, and when His side was pierced with a spear, blood and water spilled out

Each of those circumstances would and do happen to any of us in the same situations. And the final fleshly result – He died. His body stopped functioning. If His flesh was incorruptible, I don't think He *could* have died or possibly even could have bled. Yes, John 10:18 says that no one took His life from Him – He gave it willingly, but that does not change the fact that it *did* happen in the same way it would with any of us.

Let's look at other Scriptural passages that might reveal more about the flesh of the Lord Jesus.

Possibly the most confusing is *Philippians 2:5-8*:

> Have this mind among yourselves, which is yours in Christ Jesus, who, though He was in the form of God, did not count equality with God a thing to be grasped, but emptied Himself, by taking the form of a servant, being born in the likeness of men. And being found in human form, He humbled Himself by becoming obedient to the point of death, even death on a cross.

A more preferable arrangement of the words of verse 5 is found in the New American Standard version, "Have this attitude in yourselves which was also in Christ Jesus." The attitude of the Lord Jesus was willingness to accomplish for mankind what mankind could not accomplish for ourselves. But the issue of His flesh might seem clouded by words like "taking the form of," or "in the likeness of," or "in human form." But don't let that confuse you. It also says in verse 6, that He "existed in the form of God." So, God led Paul to poetically record this inspired message, which means that although Jesus was God, He did not hold on to being God, but became a human being – walked, lived, and looked like a human being. And further, as a human being in full submission to God, He underwent death – horrible death – in obedience to God's plan.

Another passage addressing His flesh – *John 1:14.*

> And the Word became flesh and dwelt among us, and we have seen His glory, glory as of the only Son from the Father, full of grace and truth.

Not only did the Lord Jesus, the living Word of God, become flesh, He dwelt among us *in* His flesh. And as a result of living among us in His flesh, we have seen His glory. That doesn't necessarily tell us that His flesh was the same or different from ours, but it does make it clear that He lived among *us*, mankind, as a human being.

Finally, look in Hebrews 2.

> For it was fitting that He [God the Father], for whom and by whom all things exist, in bringing many sons [us] to glory, should make the founder of their salvation [the Lord Jesus Christ] perfect through suffering. For He who sanctifies and those who are sanctified all have one source [or "are all one"]. (Hebrews 2:10,11)

Jesus is the one who sanctifies, and we are the ones sanctified by Him. Both He and we receive that sanctification from one source: God Himself. The suffering of Jesus made Him the complete and perfect sacrifice for sin. His earthly righteousness (sanctification) came through and from the Father. Our earthly righteousness (sanctification) comes through and from Jesus Christ from the Father.

Now, *Hebrews 2:14-18:*

Since therefore the children share in flesh and blood, He Himself likewise partook of the same things, that through death He might destroy the one who has the power of death, that is, the devil, and deliver all those who through fear of death were subject to lifelong slavery. For surely it is not angels that He helps, but He helps the offspring of Abraham [those who believe God like Abraham did, Romans 9]. Therefore, He had to be made like His brothers *in every respect*, so that He might become a merciful and faithful high priest in the service of God, to make propitiation for the sins of the people. For because He Himself has suffered when tempted, He is able to help those who are being tempted.

I don't think it can be stated more clearly than the writer of Hebrews states it. Jesus partook of the same things as we did – flesh and blood, suffering and temptation. He partook of those things to destroy the devil and the devil's power over mankind which is the fear of death. Remember Adam and Satan? "Has God surely said, 'You will die?'" The devil's primary weapon has been made null and void through the death of Jesus Christ and His subsequent resurrection. In order for the sacrifice of Jesus to be satisfactory, He had to *be* what we *are* – flesh and blood. And that's what He was. He is a merciful and faithful high priest, representing us before God through His sacrifice. His suffering through temptation in the flesh allows Him to help us when we are tempted.

The Lord Jesus went through His human life as a human being precisely the way God has always desired human beings to go through life – fully dependent on Him. And, from what we saw in John 17, the Lord Jesus expects that you and I can be one with

Him as He was one with the Father. That's the plan of God. In fact, that's God's *only* plan, so it has to work.

Did Jesus have an unfair advantage over us because He did not have a sin nature? No. Did He have an unfair advantage over us because His flesh was different than ours? No. In order for Him to take our place and satisfy the requirements of God for the removal of sin, He had to be like us. And He was. Even though He did not sin during His earthly life, when He was on the cross, He did take upon Himself and carry *all* the sin of *all* mankind throughout *all* of history. As we mentioned before, He experienced separation from God on the cross. Everything humanity experiences because of sin, He experienced as a human being. And He experienced it all at the same time. This helps us to know Him and love Him for who He is. And now, Hebrews 2:11, we share in the righteousness of God just as Jesus did because we put our trust in Him.

There is one more thing that relates to this unfair advantage issue. Second Corinthians 5:17 tells us, "If anyone is in Christ, he is a new creation. Old things have passed away, behold, all things have become new." God does not exaggerate. When He says, "all things have become new," He means *all* things. When Jesus died on the cross and paid the penalty for our sin, how much sin did He pay for? Most of us would readily answer, "All of it." And that is right. When Jesus paid the penalty for all our sin, how much sin did He leave *UN*paid? None of it. It is all paid for.

Okay – when a person believes and is in Christ, old things have passed away and all things become new. How many old things have passed away? A few? Some? Most? Think carefully – if *all* things become new, then *all* old things must have passed away. If your Bible version uses the words "sinful nature" in describing a follower of Jesus, that implies that something old was left *in* that follower of Jesus. *NOT* all things were made new.

If our minds are being renewed and our lives are being transformed, we have to deal with this. And if our preferred version of the Bible inserts someone's mistaken doctrinal understanding by substituting two words for one – "sinful nature" for "flesh" – we are fighting a battle that does not have to be fought. Does a believer in Jesus Christ have a sin nature? Every human being is born in sin, so we all start out that way. When Jesus Christ moves in through the *HOLY* Spirit of God, does He clean up most things, but leaves just a little bit of the old self there? That's ridiculous and impossible. That does not jibe with Scripture. And not merely 2 Corinthians 5:17, old things passed away, all things new. If we say that Jesus saves us from sin, it *has* to mean that He replaces what was dead with what is alive. He raises us from the dead. When a believer believes, our nature is changed. Does a believer in Jesus Christ have a sin nature? The answer is clearly, NO.

> "**His divine power** has granted to us **all things that pertain to life and godliness**, **through the knowledge of Him** who called us to His own glory and excellence, by which **He has granted to us** His precious and very great promises, so that **through them you may become partakers of the divine nature**, having **escaped from the corruption that is in the world** because of sinful desire." (2 Peter 1:3,4)

Through knowing Jesus Christ, who has called *us* to *His* own glory and excellence, and by the fact that He has granted to *us* His amazing promises, we can become partakers of the *divine* nature, having escaped from the corruption that is in the world because of sinful desire. Do you realize what Peter just said?! *Through Christ, we receive God's nature as ours* – even while still on earth. Don't misunderstand – we do not become God or gods. He comes into us, through the indwelling Spirit, living the life of Jesus Christ, who always does what the Father does and says what the Father says. We receive the fullness of God. And just like Adam was originally, and just like Jesus, our nature now is holy.

Look again at *Ephesians 2:1-6:*

> And **you were dead** in your trespasses and sins in which **you once walked**, following the course of the world, following the prince of the power of the air, the spirit that is now at work in the sons of disobedience – among whom **we all once lived in the passions of our flesh**, carrying out the desires of the body and the mind, and **were by nature children of wrath**, like the rest of mankind. **But God**, being rich in mercy, because of His great love with which He loved us, even when we **were dead** in our trespasses, **made us alive together with Christ** – by grace you have been saved – and raised us up with Him and seated us with Him in the heavenly places in Christ Jesus.

You were by nature children of wrath – our nature was once children of wrath, but *now* God has made us *alive* together *with* Christ. Although the Greek word for "sin" is not in verse 3, the Greek word for "nature" is actually in that verse (*phusis*). God changed our nature to the nature of Christ. The nature Christ has is the nature believers in Jesus now have through the power of God. And God did this *so that* He might show in *us* the immeasurable riches of His grace in kindness toward us in Christ Jesus. God desires our lives to show Him and His work and that happens to human beings in Christ.

Jump down to *Ephesians 2:18-22.*

"For through Him we both [Jew and Gentile] **have access in one Spirit to the Father.** So then, you are no longer strangers and aliens, but you are fellow citizens with the saints and members of the household of God, built on the foundation of the apostles and prophets, Christ Jesus Himself being the cornerstone, in whom the whole structure, being joined together, grows into a holy temple in the Lord. In Him, you also are being **built together into a dwelling place for God by the Spirit.**"

There is no room in that structure for a sin nature. Through Christ living in us, we now have access to God the Father by the Spirit. We have become fellow citizens with the saints – meaning we *ARE* saints – and members of the household of God. And in addition to that, *in* Christ, you, me, we also are being built together into a dwelling place for God by the Spirit.

4. Then why do I sin?!

I have included all this discussion of sin nature because it is vital to understand and know the truth. It is not semantics, whether we call it "sin nature" or "flesh." God knows the words for "sin" and "nature" and "flesh." He used the word for "flesh." This makes a tremendous difference to understand *why* I sin. Sin nature obligates human beings to sin – it would be their nature. For those who are not yet saved, it *IS* their nature. But as we have seen over and over in Scripture after Scripture, sin is *not* the nature of those who have put their faith in Jesus Christ. So, I *don't* sin because my sin nature made me sin. I sin because I *allow* sin to control my flesh. Sin is not my nature, sin is at work in my flesh. In Romans 7 Paul defines in verse 18 what he means in verse 17 by "within me", "that is, in my flesh." If your Bible version substitutes the words "sinful nature" where the Greek clearly says "flesh," cross out "sinful nature" and write "flesh" there. You're not changing the Bible. You're fixing a mistaken and inaccurate translation and putting it back to what God actually said. When sin appeals to my flesh and I give in, I stop believing Jesus Christ and start believing myself. I fall into the same trap Adam fell into. We have a sin-free nature in Christ, but we also continue to deal with the flesh. A sin-free nature is not what it takes to live free from sin. A relationship with God through Jesus Christ – Him living His life in you – Him having control of our flesh in any and every circumstance (Romans 6:13) is what it takes. So, *my* responsibility is to obey Him, trust Him, do what He says because I know Him and love Him, and to allow Him to do His work in me.

> Therefore, my beloved, as you have always obeyed, so now, not only as in my presence but much more in my absence, work out your salvation with fear and trembling, for it is **God who works in you**, both to will and work **for His good pleasure**. (Philippians 2:12,13)

Yes, I am saying that believers in Jesus Christ do not have a sin nature any longer. And I can say it confidently, because that's what God says. Read Romans 5 through 8. Read 1 John. Read Ephesians. Read the whole Bible! When a human being is free from sin and allows Jesus Christ to live His life in that person, depending fully on Him, sin becomes a foreign intrusion, something outside of the person's *true* identity. It is like a virus that cannot be tolerated. When sin raises its ugly head, we are no longer required to do what it says. "Do not *let* sin reign in your mortal body to obey *its* lusts" (Romans 6:12). When faced with temptation, we have Jesus Christ – not only our Advocate when we have sinned, but our high priest when we are tempted by sin – who helps us reject sin and trust God just as He did.

There are more questions, reservations, and concerns that could be addressed. I feel that these are the most common and most unsettling. The Lord is extremely clear in His answers to these concerns. We can and we MUST trust in the Lord with all our hearts and not lean on our *own* understanding. In all our ways, we must acknowledge Him, and He will make our paths straight (Proverbs 3:5,6). To acknowledge means to put God in His rightful place in our thinking – Master and Lord. God knows and sees and understands all. He can be trusted. We know and see and understand what we *think* we know and see and understand. And often, we get things wrong. Our trust must be in the trustworthy One alone. Once again, this is a Romans 12:1,2 issue: be transformed by the renewing of your mind!

CHAPTER 7
Conclusions

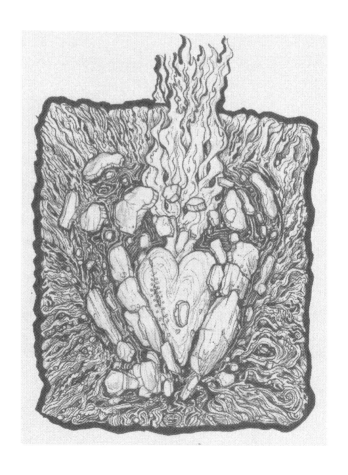

If our lives are saved by the resurrected life of the Lord Jesus, and our mortal bodies are made alive by the indwelling Spirit, what does that really imply?

Stop Trying!

Could it be that God's plan for rescuing mankind through the life, death, and resurrection of Jesus Christ, and the indwelling Spirit of God in believers, means that the life Jesus lived is the life we *all* can live – *each of us*? From what we see and hear from Jesus and the apostles and the writers of the New Testament, and even the OLD Testament, I think that is *exactly* what God's plan is. But – BUT! – I am *not* talking about us, you or me, *TRYING* to gut out the Christian life, *TRYING* to produce the life of Christ. I would guess that most of us, if we're honest, have pretty much proven we *cannot* do it. And that may have been a source of real disappointment, discouragement, frustration, and disgust throughout life. Let me set your mind at ease right now: You cannot do it. *STOP TRYING!*

Most pastors would be hesitant to tell their congregations to stop trying to be good Christians, to stop trying to live the Christian life. I'm not saying this proudly, but confidently, unless we stop *trying* to live it and allow the only one who *can* live it *to live* it, we will continue to be disappointed, discouraged, frustrated and disgusted. Trying to live the Christian life is a losing battle. It cannot happen.

Mike and Mike

I compare it to an illustration I heard a long time ago. In my day, Michael Jordan was the greatest basketball player anyone had ever seen or known or heard about. What if I, past-middle-aged-white-guy-with-too-much-extra-weight, decided that I wanted to play basketball like Michael Jordan. Could I do it? Clearly, the answer is, "No." Truthfully, Michael has moved past the ability to do it himself, but let's pretend he still could do it and I wanted to play like Mike. How could I attempt to make that happen?

I could spend hours and hours watching replays of every game he ever played. I could take copious notes on what I saw in his movements and his actions. I could study those notes daily until I knew them by heart. Should I go out on the court and give it a shot? Could I play like Michael Jordan? The answer is still, "No."

What if I went to Michael's house, knocked on the door and asked if I could spend time with him, talking about and hearing from him *how* he plays, taking even more copious notes, so as to not miss a single detail. Michael then describes his basketball ways to me, I read and re-read, study, and memorize every detail. Would I be able to play basketball like Michael Jordan at that point? No. Still not.

While sitting and listening, and taking copious notes, I have an idea. "Michael, could we play basketball together so you can show me your techniques personally and I can even copy and mimic your movements and thinking and actions?" So, we do. We head to his court and play. We play for hours and hours, all the time, me watching, imitating, *trying* to play like Mike. At the end of long sessions of lay-ups, breakaways, pull-up shots, charging the basket, ball-handling – everything that Michael does so well – would I *then* be able to play basketball like Michael Jordan? The answer is NO. Me trying to play like Michael Jordan will never work.

You know, I might – MIGHT (doubtful) – improve my basketball skills if I did all this, but the *only* way for me to be able to play like Mike would be – kind of weird, but go with me on this – if

Michael Jordan unzipped my body, climbed inside, zipped back up, and played basketball through me. Then it would be *him* playing, and not me. Then I would know him in a way I could not know him before. I would abide in his basketball abilities, and he would dwell in me. That would be the only way for Michael Wolfe to play basketball like Michael Jordan.

Do you see the connection? Michael playing ball in me – Jesus Christ living *His* life *in* me – *in you*. And in the case of Jesus Christ living His life in you and me, that actually *CAN* happen! In fact, that is precisely God's plan for mankind's existence.

In Christ – Christ In

Listen to what God clearly says in His Word about this issue (I am emphasizing the word "in" to help us see how it works):

> To them [God's saints in the church, vss 24 & 26] God chose to make known how great among the Gentiles are the riches of the glory of this mystery [hidden for ages and generations, v 26], **which is Christ IN you, the hope of glory."** (Colossians 1:27)

> I have been crucified with Christ. It is no longer I who live, **but Christ who lives IN me.** And the life I now live in the flesh **I live by faith IN the Son of God,** who loved me and gave Himself for me. (Galatians 2:20)

> I do not ask for these only, but also for those who will believe in Me through their word (you and me, remember) that they may all be one, **just as You, Father, are IN Me, and I IN You,** that they

> also **may be one IN Us**, so that the world may
> believe that You sent Me. The glory that You have
> given Me I have given to them, that they may be
> one even as We are one. **I IN them and You IN
> Me,** that they may become perfectly one, so that
> the world may know that You sent Me. (John
> 17:20-23)

If the life of Jesus Christ is to be seen during our time on earth, it
has to be demonstrated and lived by the only one who can do it –
Him. I cannot live Michael Jordan's life. I can't even play basketball
like him. How could I even try to live the rest of his life? Michael
Jordan is the only one who can live Michael Jordan's life. In the
same way, I cannot live the life of Jesus Christ – nor can you. He is
the only one who can live His life. How could I even *try* to live His
life? And, as seen in these three passages, that is precisely God's
plan – *JESUS IN US LIVING HIS LIFE.*

When we grasp this truth, it becomes more and more important
that we understand terms like "submit," "yield," "humble yourself,"
and "trust." And a key passage that we have to deal with relating
to *those* terms is *Matthew 16:24,25*:

> If anyone would come after Me, let him deny
> himself and take up his cross and follow Me.
> For whoever would save his life will lose it, but
> whoever loses his life for My sake will find it.

I know, because I have suffered with this difficulty, too, that
submitting/yielding/humbling myself and trusting Jesus and
denying myself are impossible. And the impossibility quotient
goes up as we, as I, *try* to do it. Of those four terms, the closest one
to a positive connotation is "trust." The rest might have negative
connotations to a lot of us. Most of us are fairly independent

and proud. Submission does not come easily to independent and proud people. Nor does yielding. When we take an on-ramp to a highway, typically we try to beat the car already on the road and get in front of it rather than slow down a little and slip in behind. "Yield" seems to imply defeat. "Humbling" implies me not getting first place. Certainly "deny" sounds negative. To say "no" to self is not natural.

"Trust" seems more positive. But really, all these terms are (1) biblical (although "yield" is not technically used), (2) commands of Jesus, and (3) positive in their results. The Bible uses each of these terms as commands for those who claim to know and love Jesus, who claim to be followers of Jesus, and who desire the life God promises by faith. "If you love Me, you will keep my commands," Jesus says (John 14:15,23; 15:10 and more). Do you – do I – truly believe Jesus when He commands us to do something? Or do we just *say* we believe Him? "Submit yourselves to God" (James 4:7). This is preceded by the fact that God opposes the proud. Submit yourself! And then, it is followed by "humble yourselves," with the promise that God will exalt you as you obey that command. Once again, God's ways are nearly always opposite of ours. Connecting these thoughts with "deny self, take up your cross, and follow Jesus," – it sure seems like God is saying something that is quite different than what we have experienced so far.

So, what if submitting and humbling self and denying self – trusting Jesus – allows Him to live *in* us? What needs to happen in us – in you, in me – to bring that into our existence?

Our lives need the transformation of God as He renews our minds – our understanding – and replaces it with *His* understanding as He lives His life in us. As we submit to and yield to and trust Him and deny ourselves, we get to *know* Him. Knowing Him is eternal life. Knowing Him for who He is and what He has done for our salvation and resurrection from death to life brings the transformation we need.

Growth in Knowing

Knowing Jesus is a life-long pursuit and process. Remember *Romans 1:16,17*:

> I am not ashamed of the gospel, for it is God's power for salvation to those who believe, to the Jew first and also to the Greek. For in it, the righteousness of God is revealed **from faith to faith**, just as it is written, "The righteous will live by faith."

As we pursue God's design and God's way, as we go through the process of life with Jesus living His life in us, we will grow in faith AND we will see the righteousness of God more and more, "from faith to faith." It may not be immediate, but it *will* happen.

I hope this book has encouraged you to look at God's Word from a different perspective and see something that many have missed. The Christian life is not up to *us* to accomplish. It is easily accomplished by Christ, whose life it *is*. Allow God to renew your mind regarding these issues and to transform your life – your life can be His life. That's God's plan. That's God's *only* plan. When God comes up with a plan, there are no better plans. The plan *has to work*.

And Then, the Mission!

And one thing we get to be a part of as the Lord Jesus lives His life in us, is sharing the good news of this life with others. First Peter 3:15 tells us that we should always be ready to make a defense of our faith to anyone who asks for a reason for the hope that is in us. Until I saw that the life of Jesus is meant to show through *my* life, there was nothing about my life that anyone would want to know. But when Jesus Christ shows Himself through human beings, that will cause questions. We have the privilege of taking this great news to those around us.

If you remember the 3 Circles diagram in Chapter 3, the final piece is our involvement in the mission. Our mission is to share the good news of Jesus Christ living His life in mankind with the lost people around us.

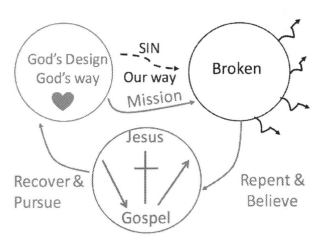

This mission is clearly the logical result of each of us realizing that Christ Himself is living *in* us. God did not save any of us because of the advantages we brought to the table. There *were* no advantages. The same is true with those around us. We probably don't see the value in people that God sees if we are living in the flesh. But if we are living in the Spirit, loving God and loving people, we can easily see that God could use them and live in them just like He uses us and lives in us. God brought each of us to Himself so that He could show Himself to the people around each of us and give those people the opportunity to be rescued and lived *in* by Jesus Christ. Our mission now is to show Jesus Christ through our lives and watch and listen and take every opportunity He gives us to supply an answer for the hope that is in us. The hope that is in us *is Christ*.

And being involved in that mission of sharing the truth of salvation by faith in Christ, and God's righteousness showing in our lives as Christ lives His life in us, now becomes much easier than before we understood God's plan. When I was a young, first-year Bible college student (1979 or 1980 – prior to hearing Major Thomas or reading *Birthright*), I had to take a class called "Personal Evangelism." I'm sure the dear professor who taught it shared with us the motivation and urging of God to share our faith, but I had not seen Jesus Christ living His life in me. I didn't even realize that was the point. Our assignment each week was to go out and share the gospel with people, using various methods and tools. This was years before I ever heard of the 3 Circles, too.

That class was a disaster for me. Evangelism of that kind does not come easily to me – starting up spiritual conversations with people I don't know. I felt like *they* would feel like I was cramming it down their throats. I think I felt that way because, even though I had been saved, I had not seen the reality of Christ *in* me, so when I was challenged, I had nothing to defend. So, I started lying about completing the assignments, and ended up having a really bad attitude about personal evangelism – not only the class, but the activity.

When anyone realizes that the Christian life is Jesus Christ *in* that person, Him doing the work, Him showing up and being Himself, then there is a lot to defend and to share in testimony with people. Read 1 Corinthians 15:3-8 and recognize that Paul is laying out the basics of the gospel message: Christ died for our sins according to the Scripture, He was buried, He was raised on the third day, according to the Scriptures. Then, He was seen by lots of people. And then Paul includes, *I have seen Him.* Paul's testimony of the living Jesus was an important part of the gospel message. As Jesus Christ lives His life *in* us, we experience Him at work and can share with those around us, "*I have seen Him alive!*"

One further thing about our mission: Jesus Christ living His life in a human being will not sin. As we share that truth with people and as they see the immense difference between their lives and Him living in us (to God's glory), we might be able to remind people that Jesus Christ does not excuse sin. He is not okay with His people practicing sin (Chapter 4 of this book and 1 John). God's grace and Jesus Christ living His life in human beings ought to move people far away from sin. As we mentioned, sin should be like a virus or a foreign object to us. Knowing Jesus and knowing the Father who sent Him will cause us to seek to move as far away from sin as we can.

Defining Sin

This message, in today's post-modern, post-Christian world, may not go over well. But remember, God is the only one who has the right and authority to define sin. His definition of sin in general, and specific sins, has never changed. It does not matter what the world says in *its* ways, 1 John 2:15-17. The world does not have that right. In fact, neither do believers. Those who make a practice of sinning do not know the Father. Just because the world now thinks some sins are acceptable and right does not make it good, acceptable, or right. We trust God, not mankind and not the world's system.

It is not our job to argue people into the faith or twist their arms or overwhelm them by our brilliance. None of that will work – one of them isn't even reality. Our job is to *love* people in their brokenness. That's God's design and God's way. That's how God used people in our lives before we came to Him. We cannot look down on the lost. Our job in this mission is to allow Jesus Christ to be seen and heard through us, and to share with those around us the hope that is in us. The Spirit of God does the work of convicting of sin, righteousness, and judgment (John 16:8-11). Our part is to show Him, to demonstrate the image of God, and to allow Jesus Christ to be Himself in us. Our job is to let people around us know that the life of Jesus in *them* is available to them.

The mission takes on much more effectiveness when the missionary has real stuff to talk about and share. Be involved in the mission of taking the message of restoration to God through Christ to the broken world around you.

One more thing: Major Thomas often included what our ultimate response can now be to the indwelling life of Jesus Christ. No matter what situation, difficulty, terror, joy, blah-ness occurs, our response to Jesus living His life in us can always be, "Thank You! Thank You, Lord Jesus that I get to see You *be* You in me. Thank You, that I can trust You regardless of the difficulty or ease of any situation. Thank You that You are sufficient in all things. Thank You!"

Amen – may it be so *in US*. **CHRIST IN YOU, THE HOPE OF GLORY**.

Appreciation

I never thought that I could write a book. I don't even really like to read. But now that I have written this, I'm begging everyone to read it! What I am presenting here is vital to life as God designed life to be. In return for you reading this book, I will be reading more – so I'm not as much of a hypocrite as I used to be …

There are people who have had a tremendous impact on my life that I want to express appreciation to and for. You might not know them, kind of like many of the people in Romans 16, where Paul includes the names of a lot of people we have never heard of before, but they were significant to Paul and to the spread of the gospel. These people have been and are significant to me. Especially concerning bringing this book into existence. Obviously, the Lord Jesus Himself is first. That almost goes without saying. But I *wanted* to say it, because He *is* the reason I felt like this book had to be written. Thank You, Lord!

As of 2018, when this was written, for 36 years, I have had a beautiful, godly, smart, and intense partner in life and ministry – my wife Connie Wolfe. She has been with me through times of ease and times of difficulty. She has been exactly who God knew I needed in those years. I have, recently (about 20 years in), discovered that she is God's gift to me to help me be the kind of man He wants me to be. I need her. I need her insights and arguments. I need her perspective and understanding. She helped me think through each point in this book as it was being formulated. Thank you, Connie – I love you!

Our children have been a great joy in our lives and our partners in ministry since before we planted Plattsmouth Bible Church in 1998. Now, as adults, they love and serve the Lord and love and serve others in various locations. Their perspectives on life and faith have been a great encouragement to Connie and me. Thank you, Caitlin, Mairin, and Brian. Thank you, Brian, for the perfect cover art for the book. And now too, thank you to Josh, Mairin's husband, who was part of our church family in Plattsmouth. I love and appreciate you all very much.

As mentioned in the book, I believed in Jesus in 1976, followed soon after by my parents and sisters. I appreciate Gary and Pam Wolfe, my parents, for their devotion to Jesus and to the things of God during my teen years up to today. I am always encouraged on Sunday mornings when they drive 75 miles to be part of the Plattsmouth Bible Church family. I am thankful for the consistency and devotion to Jesus as we have grown together as His people. I am also grateful to my sister Jan and her husband Mando, and my sister Jenny and her husband Joe, for the impact and devotion to Jesus I see in all of them. They are growing followers of Jesus and encourage me every day. Thank you, all!

Connie's mother, Ella Jane Medlin, who went to be with Jesus in 1983, also receives thanks. She and Connie's dad, Welton Medlin, who passed on prior to my introduction to Connie, raised this girl who has become such a wonderful partner, model, teacher, and follower of Jesus. Jane taught Connie and her sister, Jackie, service and loyalty, and trust in Jesus. Thank You, Lord, for Welton and Jane!

And speaking of Jackie, I am thankful for Jackie and her husband Tony – my sister-in-law and brother-in-law for 36 years. Tony and Jackie have consistently served the Lord and His people – even in times of difficulty. I told Tony once, and it is still true, that I am extremely respectful of his devotion to Jesus and God's people as a man who is a laborer in a difficult trade. He led youth groups, has served in church leadership, leads a small group, he and Jackie host people in their home, all for the furtherance of the Kingdom of God. Thank you, Jackie and Tony!

During those early days of faith for my family there were friends from the Salt Cellar coffeehouse in Atlantic, Iowa, who had major impact on our early growth as followers of Jesus. Thank you, to Cherie Carl, Cindi Metzger (two women whom the Lord used to bring me to Christ), Hal & Jude Stevenson, Duane & Alice Brown, Stephe Williams, Mark & Jody Stevenson, Lori Slutz, David Britson, Bill Davis, and all of the other young people in the Now Disciples with whom I traveled and sang and shared and lived. Thanks to the members of the band Damascus, whose music spoke Jesus to me in my first days as a Jesus follower.

In the early days of my walk with God, He brought other young men and older people into my life to put me in the place He wanted. I have shared about Major W. Ian Thomas and the impact that his ministry has had on me. But there were people with whom I spent much time and whom God used to form and mold – to transform and renew – my mind and life.

Thank you to the family at Plattsmouth Bible Church, and our previous church family of Pleasantview Berean Church. Thanks to the elders, leaders, pastors, and overseers of those churches – especially Greg Zamora, one of my longest-lasting friends and co-laborers, and his wife Evis, Tom Catlett, Dan Wehrbein, Mike McKnelly, James Jost, David F. Newell, Dave J. Newell, the pastors and leaders of the Berean Fellowship of Churches current, moved on, and passed on. Thanks to Dr. Mike Huber, David Kaufmann, Lee Cordell, Jared Totten, Sean Brandt, Jason Purdy, Tristen Davis, Jordan Watkins, Skeeter Gordon, Micah Lanham – all of you who have talked to, encouraged, approached, argued with, confronted, and always loved me.

Acknowledgements

Thank you to:

- Frank Van Campen (and Luana) for filling the pulpit and caring for the PBC family during our sabbatical. God put the right man in the right place for the right purpose.
- Mark Juntunen (and Nancy), Joe Costantino (and Carolyn), Trace Frahm (and Claudia), Doug Young, Greg Friesen, Gary Ranfeld, Dave Schellenberg, Steve Sorenson (and Mary), Bob Stevenson (and Sherry). This group of guys began this journey with me back in the early 1980s as we read and studied and taught *Birthright* by David Needham and worked through the works of Major Thomas
- Graham Stamford
- Rocky Mountain Bible Church and Linda Marvin, administrative assistant
- Those who edited and proofread - Connie Wolfe, Jan Rosales, Jenny Claggett, Judy Marnin, Janet Sharpe, and Linda Sarver

The Bible version I used in this book is most often the English Standard Version (ESV). If some other version was used, I have made note of the version quoted. Also, I am using capital letters for the personal pronouns of God. I think it makes understanding easier.

May God use this book to revolutionize your life as He has and continues to revolutionize mine. May He be seen in you. If you have lived with an understanding of Christ in you, may you be encouraged to continue to enjoy living in it and proclaiming it to those God brings to your path. I submit this book to you for the glory of God through Jesus Christ. For Jesus Christ – His glory – and the expansion of His Kingdom!

Michael Wolfe
July 7, 2018

Study Guide

Introduction

1. Explain your understanding of the kind of life God wants human beings to live.
2. "If the Lord Jesus lives His life in you, you don't even have to try to live His life – He lives it."

   Have you struggled with trying to live the Christian life? Share your frustrations and/or disappointments.

3. Have you considered that Jesus Christ lived a fully human life – a *real* human life? What's your initial response to the statement, " …and now He calls us to live the same kind of life He lived, a *real* human life"?

Chapter 1 – The Basis

1. Why does God alone, the Creator, have the right to define a real human life?
2. What could explain the statements of Jesus in John 5:19 and John 8:28,29 – " …the Son can do nothing on His own …" " …I do nothing on My own authority …"?
3. Read Philippians 2:5-7 and Hebrews 2:14-18. How much of His God-ability did Jesus put to use in His human life?

4. What is your response to the statement on page 6 that "Jesus Christ was the only real human being ever"?
5. When a person is rescued from fire or drowning or some other danger, is his/her salvation to eternal life or something else?
6. Discuss the statement, "Every moment after that moment is a moment that would not have happened if the person's life had not been saved."
7. When does salvation occur – at the moment of being saved, every moment after that, at some moment in the future, all of those?

Chapter 2 – Christ In You

1. Have you asked, "Why do I not see the evidence of Jesus Christ in me?" Share your thoughts.
2. When sharing the gospel with others, if you have, have the two parts of the gospel in Romans 1:16,17 been part of your explanation?

   What are they?
   Why are both important?
   Why is God's righteousness key?

3. Discuss what Christ can do to produce God's righteousness.
4. Read the following passages and list what believers have in Christ:

   Ephesians 1:3-5
   Ephesians 1:7-14
   Ephesians 1:15-23
   How much of what we have in Christ depends on our work, our goodness, our effort?

Who is the focus of Ephesians 1?

5. Ephesians 1:18ff – If God desires to put the same power to use in you that He used to raise Christ from the dead, what are the implications for your life?

Have you seen that kind of power at work in your life?
If not, what do you think stops it?

Chapter 3 – How Do You Get Christ In You?

1. Share how you became a believer in Jesus Christ – the circumstances and experiences.
2. Share what you have seen Jesus do in your life in the past month.
3. Take time to go to You Tube and search for "3 Circles (Gospel presentation, Ray Vaughn)." Copy down the presentation for yourself and then practice sharing it with others in your group.
4. For Christ in you to work, Christ has to be in you. Does your life, and do your actions, show obedience to God in all areas?
5. What is the solution if your answer is, "No"?
6. Discuss how you have been trying to fix your sin problems by your own power.

How can Christ in you be effective in those areas?

Chapter 4 – You're Going to Want This Chapter to Never End (Part One)

1. Read 1 John 1:5-10. Without reading into what is said, what does it actually say about light and darkness, truth and lies, being in Him or not?

2. First John 1:9 – If we confess our sins, He is faithful and just to forgive us our sins and to cleanse us from all unrighteousness.

   When were all sins paid for?
   How many sins is God holding against us?
   What does confession mean?
   Does 1 John 1:9 say that we are not forgiven until we confess our sins?
   Discuss the tension in all these questions.

3. 1 John 2:1 – what is one reason John wrote this letter?
4. Compare 1 John 1:10 with 1 John 2:1.

   Can a believer live without sin or not?
   Discuss that tension.

5. Read Mark 15:34. Why is this desperate question of the Lord Jesus so significant?
6. 1 John 2:3 – " …we know that we have come to know Him if we keep His commandments."

   If Romans 3:19,20 is true – no one is justified by the works of the Law – but we know that we know Him by keeping His commandments, what does that imply about HOW we have kept His commandments?

7. Read 1 John 2:5,6. Can you say that you know Him because your life looks like His?
   What is the only valid explanation for our lives looking exactly like the life of Jesus Christ?

Chapter 4 – You're Going to Want This Chapter to Never End (Part Two)

1. How could you be described as an idol worshiper? Read 1 John 2:15-17 for help.

2. The dramatic contrast given in 1 John 2:15,16 could be discouraging – "If anyone loves the world, the love of the Father is not in him."

   How do Christians pad or soften loving the world?
   How do you do that?
   Why is that dangerous?

3. Discuss things that tempt you and relate them to "lust of the flesh," "lust of the eyes," and "the pride of life."

   How do these things stand in opposition to the greatest and second greatest commandments? (Matthew 22:34-40)

4. Read 1 John 2:28,29. What does it mean to "abide in Him?"

   How will not abiding in Him cause shame at His coming?

5. Read 1 John 3:4-10. List the phrases in this passage that make you uncomfortable and then discuss why with the group.

   Which of these phrases is not true?
   What does your answer to the previous question imply?

6. Personal reflection question (unless you want to discuss it with the group): What does regular, consistent sin in your life reveal?

   What needs to happen in you if you see regular, consistent sin?

Chapter 4 – You're Going to Want This Chapter to Never End (Part Three)

1. Read 1 John 3:9,10. What kept Jesus from sin, according to these verses?
2. What keeps believers from sin now according to these verses?
3. How is it possible for human beings to be born of God in the same way Jesus was?
4. How is "Christ in you," "Him in us," related to being "born of God."
5. Read 1 John 4:17. What does this say specifically to believers in Jesus Christ?
6. Reflect on what you have discussed so far in this study. What difference do these things make in your daily life?

Chapter 5 – More Truth to Celebrate (Part One)

1. Have you ever asked, "Why doesn't Christ in me work for ME?"

   OR

   Have you felt like you didn't have enough faith to live that way?
   What caused you to ask questions like that?

2. What's your response to "Jesus lived the way He calls us to live?" (page 45)
3. How did Jesus live human life? What factor energized His human life? Is it really the same thing for us?
4. Read Philippians 2:7. If Jesus emptied Himself of His abilities as God while on earth, how does that show His total dependence on the Father in every circumstance?
5. Read John 14:8-14. How can verse 12 be true?
6. Read Genesis 1:27. How is it that God's image can be seen in us?

Chapter 5 – More Truth to Celebrate (Part Two)

1. What have you thought when saying, "In Jesus' name" at the end of prayer?
2. According to John 14:8-14, what does asking "in Jesus' name" imply?
3. How can a person know what glorifies the Father through the Son?
4. Discuss times of suffering in your life and how God was or could be glorified.
5. Read Romans 12:1,2. How do these verses apply to Jesus asking for the Father to be glorified through Jesus's suffering?
6. What kind of suffering did Jesus face – consequences for poor choices or something else?

   How does this difference relate to you and your suffering?

7. What does it mean to "know the Father and Jesus Christ whom He sent?"

Chapter 6 – Questions/Concerns

1. What questions or concerns do you have up to this point in the book? Discuss with the group.
2. Do you see evidence of incorrect teaching in your faith? Could that incorrect teaching cause frustration? Discuss.
3. Review the ways God has provided for us to know Him (pages 60-62). What are they? Which are you neglecting? Which have you resisted? What has kept you from utilizing those provisions?
4. This book is not about us doing miracles. Explain how Jesus did miracles as a real human being. Who did the miracles?
5. Read Romans 12:1,2. What kind of issues in your mind need renewal leading to the transformation of God?
6. What is another name for seeking to do miracles? Who is supposed to be our focus?
7. How were Adam and Jesus similar? (review Genesis 1 & 2, Matthew 1 & 2, Luke 2, and Romans 5)
8. Was it easy for Jesus to resist sin – not having a sin nature?
9. What was it that kept Jesus from sinning?
10. Read the following passages. Discuss what you learn about the human flesh of Jesus Christ.

    John 1:14
    Hebrews 2:10,11
    Hebrews 2:14-18

11. Read 2 Peter 1:3,4. Discuss what "partakers of the divine nature" means.
12. "Then why do I sin?!" Most of us have this question. Discuss what the book explains from the Scripture in answer to this question (page 73 ff).

Chapter 7 - Conclusions

1. How do you react to the phrase, "Stop trying" as it relates to living a Christian life?
2. Discuss this question: If Jesus really did live His life in you, what would be different than it is now?
3. From what you have read, what must happen in you to open your life to Jesus Christ living His life in you?
4. Discuss your reaction to the words, "submit," "yield," "humble yourself," and "trust Jesus."
5. Have you considered that *Christ in* you is God's only plan and that, consequently, it has to work? Discuss this.
6. How does knowing Jesus Christ and Him living His life in you change your view of our mission and command to go and make disciples?
7. Make a private list of people with whom you find it difficult to share the good news.

Knowing the reality of Jesus Christ living His life in you and in all believers, how does your attitude about those people change? How will your prayers for them change?

Printed in the United States
By Bookmasters